MODERN SCOTTISH POETRY

THE LITTLE WHITE ROSE

The Rose of all the world is not for me.
I want for my part
Only the little white rose of Scotland
That smells sharp and sweet—and breaks the heart.

Hugh MacDiarmid

MODERN
SCOTTISH POETRY

an anthology of the
Scottish Renaissance

1925 — 1985

edited by

MAURICE LINDSAY

ROBERT HALE · LONDON

Copyright © Preface and Introduction: Maurice Lindsay
1976, 1986
For further copyrights see Acknowledgements page 19
This new edition published 1986

ISBN 0 7090 2758 3

The publisher gratefully acknowledges subsidy
from the Scottish Arts Council towards the publication
of this volume

Robert Hale Limited
Clerkenwell House
Clerkenwell Green
London EC1R 0HT

British Library Cataloguing in Publication Data

Modern Scottish poetry: an anthology of
the Scottish renaissance 1925-1985.—
4th ed.
1. Scottish poetry   2. English poetry—
Scottish authors
I. Lindsay, Maurice
821'.912'08   PR8658

Printed in Great Britain
by St. Edmundsbury Press, Bury St. Edmunds, Suffolk
and bound in Scotland by Hunter & Foulis Ltd.

CONTENTS

10   *Contents*

12 Contents

PREFACE TO THE FOURTH EDITION

When *Modern Scottish Poetry: An Anthology of the Scottish Renaissance 1925 – 45* first appeared, its purpose was to bring together for the first time work in Scots, English and Gaelic reflecting a breakthrough from the stultifying traditions of post-Burnsian sentimentality which – the grim poetry of James Thomson (B.V.) and John Davidson apart – had characterized most Scottish verse of the previous century. MacDiarmid, the revivifier (at least temporarily), of Lallans and the relentless questioner of totally accepted Scots values, together with Muir, the re-discoverer of poetic metaphysical reflectiveness, made their very different major individual contributions to the movement, as well as setting its pace and general direction. After them came a remarkably continuous and varied literary flowering. Whether or not you choose to call it a renaissance, it was undoubtedly nurtured on some sort of belief that Scotland, the nation, was strengthening its sense of identity in relation to the changing modern world. That indefinable feeling in the air, however, was rudely and quickly dispersed by the Referendum débâcle of 1979.

Perhaps the failure of any political follow-up to support the imagination of the poets would eventually have led to similar disillusion. Perhaps the whole idea of a Scottish Renaissance in the major-power world of the twentieth century could only be a last romantic throw, despite the realistic expressionism of its practitioners. Fortunately, however, it produced a substantial corpus of poetry, sharing a recognizable affinity, and easily enjoyable in its own right.

Many younger writers of the so-called 'Glasgow School', more assertive in fiction than in verse and understandably affected by mass unemployment and Scotland's depressing and seemingly irreversible general economic decline, now reflect a hopelessness, a sense of disintegration, which apparently seeks resolution in something approaching philosophic and linguistic anarchy. Clearly, literature thus motivated is of a different kind than poetry enthused by the idea of renaissance and the possibility of fulfilment. 1985 therefore seems as good a year as any in which to round off a collection embracing an easily-definable era, however it is to be labelled, in this fourth and final edition of an anthology continuously in print for all of its forty years.

As in the case of the original and subsequent editions, I have employed pit-of-the-stomach criteria. A poem had to move me, not just once but on repeated occasions, to qualify for inclusion. Exclusion, therefore, should be seen in the light of this personal reaction, except in the case of Alasdair Maclean who, most unfortunately, some years ago placed a ban on anything by him appearing in anthologies where the word 'Scotland' or 'Scottish' formed part of the title.

I am particularly glad to have been able to include, among others, two new poets — one, Valerie Gillies, already an established voice, and Robert Crawford, an exceptionally talented arrival on the scene; glad, too, to have the opportunity of restoring the correct attribution of MacDiarmid's 'The Little White Rose'. The unintentional circumstances leading to its misattribution in the Third Edition are fully set out in my autobiography *Thank You For Having Me*, and so hardly need to be recounted again here.

Maurice Lindsay
Milton Hill, Dumbarton, January 1986

INTRODUCTION

I

Scottish Poetry in the Scots tongue goes back in fragmentary form to the thirteenth century, and in English at least to the sixteenth. With the more ancient history of Gaelic poetry, which stems from central Irish traditions, we need not here precisely concern ourselves.

The two earlier outstanding periods in the Scots poetic tradition were the so-called Golden Age of the Makars, from about 1480 to 1560, and the Eighteenth-Century Revival, begun by Allan Ramsay in 1716 and outlasting James Hogg in the nineteenth century only as a protracted, weakened, coda. At the heart of the Golden Age, the saturnine, virtuostic muse of William Dunbar cavorts with native intensity, scornfully begs a living from royal patrons, or thunders out in great peals of aureate word-music. At the heart of the Eighteenth-Century Revival there is Robert Burns flaying with fast-moving, colloquial satire the petty tyrannies and hypocrisies of both the Presbyterian Church and the secular establishment, sounding abroad a clear call on behalf of human brotherliness, and celebrating the love between man and woman with a tenderness, a passion and a range of experience few other song-writers have equalled. Except for Hogg, who re-established creative contact with the old Scots kingdom of the supernatural and shared with Lady Nairne the honour of providing some of the Jacobite and other songs still most frequently sung after those of Burns, Scots-writing poets during the rest of the century were for the most part only minor figures; many of them however, contributing a single song or a poem or two, to add collective richness to this stage of our heritage. But, Stevenson apart, most nineteenth-century practitioners of Lallans (as Burns called Lowland Scots) simply sank deeper into a mire of imitative sentimentality.

The tradition of English poetry written by Scots, though in its different way distinguished, has had no such obvious outstanding flowerings. The Scottish Castalians, who wrote to entertain the courts of James VI and I and Charles I, have recently been rediscovered in the pleasing company of the music for which their verses were originally intended.

Drummond of Hawthornden reflected the cultures of France and Italy, as he polished the sweet melancholy of his verses in his wooded castle high above the Esk. Sir Walter Scott more than any other writer shored up Scotland's consciousness of her history against the threatening ruin of Anglicization, if perhaps more effectively through his novels than his long poems.

It may well seem to future generations that the third outstanding period of Scottish poetry has been the middle half of the twentieth century; those five or so decades containing the movement dubbed by Denis Saurat 'The Scottish Renaissance'. The muse of 'Hugh MacDiarmid' (C. M. Grieve) has been both its inspiration and its conscience.

Like the two previous movements, the Scottish Renaissance has had nationalistic overtones. England was the physical enemy during the reigns of the six Jameses; union with her meant union with the enemy of Scotland's cultural traditions and languages during the eighteenth and early nineteenth centuries. It is surely no accident that the Scottish Renaissance, though making use of European ideas and literary innovations, has sought to strengthen both Scots and Gaelic for literary purposes, and to build upon the new emotional honesty in the handling of English initiated for Scotland by the late nineteenth-century poets James Thomson (B. V.) and John Davidson. The Scottish Renaissance has also coincided with a steady strengthening of belief among several successive generations of Scots that their country should have more say in the running of her practical affairs. The purpose of this anthology, now in its third and, I hope, definitive edition, is to attempt to reflect the best work produced during the half-century it covers, as experienced through the sensibility of one man.

II

In the first edition of *Modern Scottish Poetry: An Anthology of the Scottish Renaissance*, which appeared in 1946, the work of the members of those groups known as the New Apocalypse and the Lallans Makars featured strongly. Most of these writers have subsequently written better, clearer work on their own. For the second edition, published in 1966, some essential changes were consequently made, and the work of several younger poets was added. My editorial brief then, however, was to change as little as possible.

It seems to me that the impetus of the Scottish Renaissance—though not, of course, the continuing validity of its achievement—may now be on the wane. Some of the younger writers claim to be anti-Renaissance, though not necessarily anti-Scottish. Others have evidently become caught up with rapidly changing international fashion. This, therefore, appears to be as good a moment as any to try to present as effective as possible an anthology of what the half-century or so of the Scottish Renaissance may have achieved.

Movements, whether of literature or of history, do not conform precisely to the edges of centuries or decades. In order to demonstrate the linguistic base of unsentimental honesty on which MacDiarmid's experimental Scots was founded, I have included two poems by Pittendrigh MacGillivray, who attempted, as did Lewis Spence, to resuscitate a form of Modernized Middle Scots: 'gentleman's Scots', as Spence described his language. I have also included the work of Violet Jacob and Marion Angus, who seem to me to anticipate the spirit of the new movement whilst still keeping their link with the old. At the other end of the period, I have included the work of some younger poets whose link with the Renaissance may be thought more tenuous, but who might not have written as they do had it not existed. Those whose best work is perhaps yet to come are given merely token representation. In general, I have not included the work of young writers who have not yet published a sizeable volume. The main body of the collection is devoted to Renaissance writers, who are therefore more fully represented. MacDiarmid, however, presents a special problem. The range, intellectual energy and variety of the best of MacDiarmid can no more be adequately represented in any Scottish anthology of his period than could that of Yeats in a comparable Irish volume. The purpose of the MacDiarmid selection here, therefore, is simply to show as many facets as possible of his achievement in the context of the vigorous movement he originally conceived and nursed into life.

For the rest, I have relied upon Dryden's view: 'The chief,

perhaps the only aim of poetry, is to delight.' Taking 'delight' in its broadest sense, to mean that sense of *frisson*, whether of pleasure or of pity, which a moving poem arouses, I have used Dryden's touchstone as honed against my own sensibility. To poems chosen by such a method there attaches, inevitably so far as I am concerned, a quality of memorability. Consequently, this is not—nor indeed, ever was—intended to be the kind of anthology which sets out to include everyone who has ever turned a well-made verse or dared an interesting experiment between 1925 anbd 1975. Nor have I thought it necessary to allow considerations of age, location, period of production, or choice of Scots, English or Gaelic, to hamper my sensibility in bringing to these pages its objects of delight.

Glasgow   *Maurice Lindsay*

Acknowledgements

The editor gratefully acknowledges permission from the following: Mrs Kathleen MacLellan (for the poems by Robert MacLellan), Mrs Isabella Mackie (for the poems by Albert D. Mackie), John Gray (for the poems by Sir Alexander Gray), Mrs E.A. Stapleforth (for 'Enough' by Muriel Stuart), Mrs Paddy Fraser (for the poems by G.S. Fraser), Mrs Hella Young (for the poems by Douglas Young), Michael Grieve (for the poems by Hugh MacDiarmid), Mrs Nessie Graham (for the poems by W.S. Graham) and, for their own poems, James Aitchison, Alan Bold, George Mackay Brown, George Bruce, Tom Buchan, Donald Campbell, Stewart Conn, Robert Crawford, Ian Hamilton Finlay, Robin Fulton, Valerie Gillies, Duncan Glen, Giles Gordon, Stanley Roger Green, Andrew Greig, Hamish Henderson, Alan Jackson, Tom Leonard, Liz Lochhead, Norman MacCaig, Alastair Mackie, Hamish MacLaren, Sorley Maclean, William Montgomerie, Edwin Morgan, Stephen Mulrine, Alastair Reid, Christopher Rush, R. Crombie Saunders, Alexander Scott, Tom Scott, Iain Crichton Smith, Prof. Derick S. Thomson, Sydney Tremayne, W. Price Turner.
    Permission is acknowledged from:
Jonathan Cape Ltd on behalf of the Executors of the Estate of Muriel Stuart for 'The Seed Shop' and 'In the Orchard' from *Selected Poems*; W.L. Lorimer Memorial Trust for 'Still Gyte, Man?', 'The Old Fisherman' and 'An Sealgair Agus An Aois' from *Wind Over Loch Fyne* by George Campbell Hay; John

Calder (Publishers) Ltd for 'Loch Leven', 'Largo', 'Spleen', 'The Grace of God and the Meth-Drinker', 'Elegy XIII' and 'Hamewith' by Sydney Goodsir Smith; John Murray (Publishers) Ltd for 'The Water-Hen', 'Tam i' the Kirk' and 'The Neep-Fields by the Sea' by Violet Jacob; David Higham Associates Ltd for 'About Scotland, & C.', 'Personal History: For my Son', 'It was Easier', 'Broken Arrowheads at Chilmark', Martha's Vineyard' by Ruthven Todd; Routledge & Kegan Paul PLC for 'Inverbeg', 'The Ship' and 'The Constant North' from *The Bombed Happiness* by J.F. Hendry; Carcanet Press Ltd for 'A Letter', 'Tree', 'Peterhead in May' and 'Home from Sea' by Burns Singer; Martin Secker & Warburg Ltd for 'Loch Brandy', 'The Mountain', 'In December', 'The Falls of Glomach', 'The Echoing Cliff' and 'Sudden Thaw' by Andrew Young; The Trustees of the National Library of Scotland for 'The Philosophic Taed', 'The Gowk', 'The Tryst', 'The Thocht', 'The Lanely Müne', 'Song', 'Miracle', 'Revelation' and 'The Children' by William Soutar; Faber & Faber Ltd for 'Mary's Song', 'Alas! Poor Queen' and 'Think Lang' from *The Turn of The Day* and 'Anemones' from *The Singin' Lass* by Marion Angus; 'Mary Stuart', 'Scotland 1941', 'Then', 'The Sufficient Place', 'The Little General', 'A Birthday', 'The River' and 'Scotland's Winter' from *Collected Poems* by Edwin Muir; 'Landscape with One Figure', 'Ships' and 'The Love Day' from *Terry Street*, 'The New Girls' from *The Happier Life* and 'The Harp of Renfrewshire' and 'War Blinded' from *St Kilda's Parliament* by Douglas Dunn; Gordon Wright Publishing Ltd for 'Shy Geordie' by Helen Cruickshank.

Every effort has been made to trace and acknowledge all copyright holders but the Editor offers his apologies for the inevitable omissions.

MODERN SCOTTISH POETRY

ABASSHYD

I toke hyr heid atween my hondes
   And kyste hyr dusky hair;
I lyghtly touchte hyr luvely cheek,
   Syn kyste hyr mouth so rare.

A lityll flame cam up hyr neck
   To tell hyr herte had fyre;
But, sum aschamte, wyth eyen cast down,
   Hyr mynde restrainte desyre.

A swete, pure mayde of gentyl kynd—
   A flowr ryght fayre to see:
Yet wyth ane potent gyfte of sowle
   Fro yll to keep hyr free.

Abasshte before hyr luvelyness
   I knelt and kyste hyr honde;
In token that I humbled me,
   And stayed at hyr commaunde.

MERCY O' GODE

I
Twa bodachs, I mind, had a threep ae day,
   Aboot man's chief end—
   Aboot man's chief end.
Whan the t'ane lookit sweet his words war sour,
Whan the tither leuch out his words gied a clour,
But whilk got the better I wasna sure—
   I wasna sure,
     An' needna say.

II
But I mind them well for a queer-like pair—
   A gangrel kind,

23

A gangrel kind:
The heid o' the ane was beld as an egg,
The ither, puir man, had a timmer leg,
An' baith for the bite could dae nocht but beg
    Nocht but beg—
    Or live on air!

III
On a table-stane in the auld Kirkyaird,
    They ca' 'The Houff',
    They ca' 'The Houff',
They sat in their rags like wearyfu' craws,
An' fankl't themsel's about a 'FIRST CAUSE',
An' the job the Lord had made o' His laws,
    Made o' His laws,
    In human regaird.

IV
Twa broken auld men wi' little but jaw—
    Faur better awa
    Aye—better awa;
Yawmerin' owr things that nane can tell,
The yin for a Heaven, the ither for Hell;
Wi' nae mair in tune than a crackit bell—
    A crackit bell,
    Atween the twa.

V
Dour badly he barkit in praise o' the Lord—
    'The pooer o' Gode
    An' the wull o' Gode';
But Stumpie believ't nor in Gode nor man—
Thocht life but a fecht without ony plan,
An' the best nae mair nor a flash i' the pan—
    A flash i' the pan,
    In darkness smored.

VI
Twa dune men—naither bite nor bed!—
    A sair-like thing—

24

An' unco thing.
To the Houff they cam to lay their heid
An' seek a nicht's rest wi' the sleepin' deid,
Whar the stanes wudna grudge nor ony tak' heed
    Nor ony tak' heed:
    But it's ill to read.

VII

They may hae been bitter, an' dour, an' warsh,
    But wha could blame—
    Aye—wha could blame?
I kent bi their look they war no' that bad
But jist ill dune bi an' driven half mad:
Whar there's nae touch o' kindness this life's owr sad
    This life's owr sad,
    An' faur owr harsh.

VIII

But as nicht drave on I had needs tak' the road,
    Fell gled o' ma dog—
    The love o' a dog:
An' tho nane wad hae me that day at the fair,
I raither't the hill for a houff than in there,
'Neth a table-stane, on a deid man's lair—
    A deid man's lair—
    Mercy o' Gode.

bodach—an old man   threep—conversation   clour—wallop
gangrel—tramp   heid—head   beld—bald   timmer—wooden
baith—both   for the bite—to eat   fankl't—tied themselves in a knot
regaird—regard   jaw—talk   yawmerin'—complaining   the yin—
the one   dour—glum   pooer—power   fecht—fight   smored—
smothered   sair-like—sore-like   unco—strange   warsh—without zest
ill dune bi— badly done by   fell—very   gled—glad   houff—
meeting-place   lair—grave

VIOLET JACOB

THE WATER-HEN

As I gaed doon by the twa mill dams i' the mornin'
The water-hen cam' oot like a passin' wraith,
And her voice ran through the reeds wi' a sound of warnin',
    'Faith—keep faith!'
'Aye, bird, tho' ye see but ane ye may cry on baith!'

As I gaed doon the field when the dew was lyin',
My ain love stood whaur the road an' the mill-lade met,
And it seemed to me that the rowin' wheel was cryin',
    'Forgie—forget,
And turn, man, turn, for ye ken that ye lo'e her yet!'

As I gaed doon the road 'twas a weary meetin',
For the ill words said yestreen they were aye the same,
And my het he'rt drouned the wheel wi' its heavy beatin'.
    'Lass, think shame,
It's no for me to speak, for it's you to blame!'

As I gaed doon by the toon when the day was springin'
The Baltic brigs lay thick by the soundin' quay
And the riggin' hummed wi' the sang that the wind was
    singin',
    'Free—gang free,
For there's mony a load on shore may be skailed at sea!'

   .   .   .   .   .   .

When I cam hame wi' the thrang o' the years ahint me
There was naucht to see for the weeds and the lade in spate,
But the water-hen by the dams she seemed aye to mind me,
    Cryin' 'Hope—wait!'
'Aye, bird, but my een grow dim, an' it's late—late!'

het—hot   skailed—scattered, or dropped

TAM I' THE KIRK

O Jean, my Jean, when the bell ca's the congregation
O'er valley and hill wi' the ding frae its iron mou',
When a'body's thochts is set on their ain salvation,
    Mine's set on you.

There's a reid rose lies on the Buik o' the Word afore ye
That was growin' braw on its bush at the keek o' day,
But the lad that pu'd yon flower i' the mornin's glory
    He canna pray.

He canna pray, but there's nane i' the kirk will heed him
Whaur he sits sae still his lane at the side o' the wa',
For nane but the reid rose kens what my lassie gied him—
    It and us twa.

He canna sing for the sang that his ain he'rt raises,
He canna see for the mist that's afore his een,
And a voice droons the hale o' the psalms and the
    paraphrases
        Crying 'Jean! Jean! Jean!'

THE NEEP-FIELDS BY THE SEA

Ye'd wonder foo the seasons rin
This side o' Tweed an' Tyne:
The hairst's awa'; October-month
Cam in a whilie syne,
But the stooks are oot in Scotland yet,
There's green upon the tree,
And oh! what grand's the smell ye'll get
Frae the neep-fields by the sea!

The lang lift lies abune the warld,
On ilka windless day
The ships creep doon the ocean line
Sma' on the band o' grey;
And the lang sigh heaved upon the sand

27

Comes pechin' up tae me
And speils the cliffs tae whaur ye stand
I' the neep-fields by the sea.

Oh, time's aye slow, tho' time gangs fast
When siller's a' tae mak',
An' deith, afore ma poke is fu'
May grip me i' the back;
But ye'll tak' ma banes an' my Sawbath braws,
Gin deith's ower smairt for me,
And set them up amang the shaws
I' the lang rows plantit atween the wa's,
A tattie-dulie for fleggin' craws
I' the neep-fields by the sea.

pechin'—panting   speils—climbs   poke—pocket   tattie-dulie—
scarecrow

MARION ANGUS

MARY'S SONG

I wad ha'e gi'en him my lips tae kiss,
Had I been his, had I been his;
Barley breid and elder wine,
Had I been his as he is mine.

The wanderin' bee it seeks the rose;
Tae the lochan's bosom the burnie goes;
The grey bird cries at evenin's fa',
'My luve, my fair one, come awa'.'

My beloved sall ha'e this he'rt tae break,
Reid, reid wine and the barley cake,
A he'rt tae break, and a mou' tae kiss,
Tho' he be nae mine, as I am his.

ALAS! POOR QUEEN

She was skilled in music and the dance
And the old arts of love
At the court of the poisoned rose
And the perfumed glove,
And gave her beautiful hand
To the pale Dauphin
A triple crown to win—
And she loved little dogs
  And parrots
 And red-legged partridges
And the golden fishes of the Duc de Guise
And a pigeon with a blue ruff
She had from Monsieur d'Elboeuf.

Master John Knox was no friend to her;
She spoke him soft and kind,
Her honeyed words were Satan's lure
The unwary soul to bind.

'Good sir, doth a lissome shape
And a comely face
Offend your God His Grace
Whose Wisdom maketh these
Golden fishes of the Duc de Guise?'

She rode through Liddesdale with a song:
'Ye streams sae wondrous strang,
Oh, mak' me a wrack as I come back
But spare me as I gang.'
While a hill-bird cried and cried
Like a spirit lost
By the grey storm-wind tost.

Consider the way she had to go,
Think of the hungry snare,
The net she herself had woven,
Aware or unaware,
Of the dancing feet grown still,

The blinded eyes—
Queens should be cold and wise,
And she loved little things,
    Parrots
    And red-legged partridges
And golden fishes of the Duc de Guise
And the pigeon with the blue ruff
She had from Monsieur d'Elboeuf.

THINK LANG

Lassie, think lang, think lang,
Ere his step comes ower the hill.
Luve gi'es wi' a lauch an' a sang,
An' whiles for nocht but ill.

Thir's weary time tae rue
In the lea-lang nicht yer lane
The ghaist o'a kiss on yer mou'
An' sough o' win' in the rain.

Lassie, think lang, think lang,
The trees is clappin' their han's,
The burnie clatterin' wi' sang
Rins ower the blossomy lan's.

Luve gi'es wi' a lauch an' a sang,
His fit fa's licht on the dew.
Oh, lass, are ye thinkin' lang,
Star een an' honey mou'?

ANEMONES

Anemones, they say, are out
   By sheltered woodland streams,
With budding branches all about
   Where Spring-time sunshine gleams;

Such are the haunts they love, but I
   With swift remembrance see
Anemones beneath a sky
   Of cold austerity—

Pale flowers too faint for winds so chill
   And with too fair a name—
That day I lingered on a hill
   For one who never came.

LEWIS SPENCE

PORTRAIT OF MARY STUART, HOLYROOD

Wauken by nicht, and bydand on some boon,
Glaumour of saul, or spirituall grace,
I haf seen sancts and angells in the face,
And like a fere of seraphy the moon;
But in nae mirk nor sun-apparelled noon,
Nor pleasaunce of the planets in their place,
Of luve devine haf seen sae pure a trace
As in yon shadow of the Scottis croun.

Die not, O rose, dispitefull of hir mouth,
Nor be ye lilies waefu at hir snaw;
This dim device is but hir painted sake;
The mirour of ane star of vivand youth,
That not hir velvets nor hir balas braw
Can oueradorn, or luve mair luvely make.

31

CAPERNAUM
(St Matthew XI, 23)

If aa the bluid shed at thy Tron,
    Embro, Embro,
If aa the bluid shed at thy Tron
    Were sped into a river,
It wad caa the mills o Bonnington,
    Embro, Embro,
It wad caa the mills o Bonnington
    For ever and for ever.

If aa the tears that thou has grat,
    Embro, Embro,
If aa the tears that thou has grat
    Were shed into the sea,
Whaur wad ye find an Ararat,
    Embro, Embro,
Whaur wad ye find an Ararat
    Frae that fell flude to flee?

If aa the psalms sung in thy kirks,
    Embro, Embro,
If aa the psalms sung in thy kirks
    Were gaithered in a wind,
It wad shog the taps o Roslin birks,
    Embro, Embro,
It wad shog the taps o Roslin birks
    Till time was out o mynd.

If aa the broken herts o thee,
    Embro, Embro,
If aa the broken herts o thee
    Were heapit in a howe,
There wad be neither land nor sea,
    Embro, Embro,
There wad be neither land nor sea
    But yon reid brae—and thou!

SCOTLAND

Here in the Uplands
The soil is ungrateful;
The fields, red with sorrel,
Are stony and bare.
A few trees, wind-twisted—
Or are they but bushes?—
Stand stubbornly guarding
A home here and there.

Scooped out like a saucer,
The land lies before me;
The waters, once scattered,
Flow orderedly now
Through fields where the ghosts
Of the marsh and the moorland
Still ride the old marches,
Despising the plough.

The marsh and the moorland
Are not to be banished;
The bracken and heather,
The glory of broom,
Usurp all the balks
And the fields' broken fringes,
And claim from the sower
Their portion of room.

This is my country,
The land that begat me.
These windy spaces
Are surely my own.
And those who here toil
In the sweat of their faces
Are flesh of my flesh,
And bone of my bone.

Hard is the day's task—
Scotland, stern Mother—
Wherewith at all times
Thy sons have been faced:
Labour by day,
And scant rest in the gloaming,
With Want an attendant,
Not lightly outpaced.

Yet do thy children
Honour and love thee.
Harsh is thy schooling,
Yet great is the gain:
True hearts and strong limbs,
The beauty of faces,
Kissed by the wind
And caressed by the rain.

Lairhillock, Kincardine.

HEINE IN SCOTS

There were three kings cam frae the East;
They spiered in ilka clachan:
'O, which is the wey to Bethlehem,
My bairns, sae bonnily lachin'?'

O neither young nor auld could tell;
They trailed till their feet were weary.
They followed a bonny gowden starn,
That shone in the lift sae cheery.

The starn stude ower the ale-hoose byre
Whaur the stable gear was hingin'.
The owsen mooed, the bairnie grat,
The kings begoud their singin'.

ON A CAT, AGEING

He blinks upon the hearth-rug,
  And yawns in deep content,
Accepting all the comforts
  That Providence has sent.

Louder he purrs and louder,
  In one glad hymn of praise
For all the night's adventures,
  For quiet restful days.

Life will go on for ever,
  With all that cat can wish;
Warmth and the glad procession
  Of fish and milk and fish.

Only—the thought disturbs him—
  He's noticed once or twice,
The times are somehow breeding
  A nimbler race of mice.

THE FINE FECHTIN MOUSE

'Fairest o' fair, O, hear my cry;
O, open and let your love inby;
Sae lang have I been here standin,
  Ay, ay, ay, standin,
That I'm frozen all-utterly.'

'Deed, and I winna open to ye,
Nor to ony gangrel, as weel ye may be;
But first, you maun tell me strauchtly,
  Ay, ay, ay, strauchtly,
That there's nane that you lo'e but me.'

'Dear lass, I lo'e you; weel you ken
That you've aye been the only ane.
But sae lang have I been here standin,

> *Ay, ay, ay, standin,*
> That I'm frozen cauld to the bane.'

In the nicht, in the nicht, in the middle o' the nicht,
A dunt at the winnock gae's baith a fricht.
And her mither, O ay, *she* heard it,
> *Ay, ay, ay, SHE heard it:*
'Are you sure, Jean, that a' thing's a' richt?'

'O mither, it's only Baudrons, the cat:
He's efter a moose, and that's what he's at;
And dod, but he's grippit the beastie;
> *Ay, ay, ay, the beastie—*
She's a fine fechtin moose for a' that.'

THE DEIL O' BOGIE

When I was young, and ower young,
I wad a deid-auld wife;
But ere three days had gane by,
> Gi-Ga-Gane-by,
I rued the sturt and strife.

Sae to the Kirk-yaird furth I fared,
And to the Deil I prayed:
'O, muckle Deil o' Bogie,
> Bi-Ba-Bogie,
Come, tak the runkled jade.'

When I got hame, the soor auld bitch
Was deid, ay, deid eneugh.
I yokkit the mare to the dung-cairt,
> Ding-Dang-Dung-cairt,
And drove her furth—and leuch!

And when I cam to the place o' peace,
The grave was howked, and snod:
'Gae canny wi' the corp, lads,
> Ci-Ca-Corp, lads,
You'll wauk her up, by God!

Ram in, ram in the bonnie yird
Upon the ill-daein wife.
When she was hale and herty,
   Hi-Hi-Herty,
She plagued me o' my life.'

But when I gat me hame again,
The hoose seemed toom and wide.
For juist three days I waited,
   Wit-Wat-Waited,
Syne took a braw young bride.

In three short days my braw young wife
Had ta'en to lounderin me.
'Gie's back, dear Deil o' Bogie,
   Bi-Ba-Bogie,
My auld calamitie!'

ANDREW YOUNG

LOCH BRANDY

All day I heard the water talk
From dripping rock to rock
And water in bright snowflakes scatter
On boulders of the black Whitewater;
But louder now than these
The silent scream of the loose tumbling screes.

Grey wave on grey stone hits
And grey moth flits
Moth after moth, but oh,
What floats into that silver glow,
What golden moth
That rises with a strange majestic sloth?

O heart, why tremble with desire
As on the water shakes that bridge of fire?
The gold moth floats away, too soon
To narrow to a hard white moon
That scarce will light the path
Stumbling to where the cold mist wreathes the strath.

THE MOUNTAIN

The burn ran blacker for the snow
And ice-floe on ice-floe
Jangled in heavy lurches
Beneath the claret-coloured birches.

Dark grouse rose becking from the ground
And deer turned sharp heads round,
The antlers on their brows
Like stunted trees with withered boughs.

I climbed to where the mountain sloped
And long wan bubbles groped
Under the ice's cover,
A bridge that groaned as I crossed over.

I reached the mist, brighter than day,
That showed a specious way
By narrow crumbling shelves,
Where rocks grew larger than themselves.

But when I saw the mountain's spire
Looming through that damp fire,
I left it still unwon
And climbed down to the setting sun.

IN DECEMBER

I watch the dung-cart stumble by
    Leading the harvest to the fields,
That from cow-byre and stall and stye
    The farmstead in the winter yields.

Like shocks in a reaped field of rye
    The small black heaps of lively dung
Sprinkled in the grass-meadow lie
    Licking the air with smoky tongue.

This is Earth's food that man piles up
   And with his fork will thrust on her,
And Earth will lie and slowly sup
   With her moist mouth through half the year.

THE FALLS OF GLOMACH

Rain drifts forever in this place
Tossed from the long white lace
The Falls trail on black rocks below,
And golden-rod and rose-root shake
In wind that they forever make;
So though they wear their own rainbow
It's not in hope, but just for show,
For rain and wind together
Here through the summer make a chill wet weather.

THE ECHOING CLIFF

White gulls that sit and float
Each on his shadow like a boat,
Sandpipers, oystercatchers
And herons, those grey stilted watchers,
From loch and corran rise,
And as they scream and squawk abuse
Echo from wooded cliff replies
So clearly that the dark pine boughs,
Where goldcrests flit
And owls in drowsy wisdom sit,
Are filled with sea-birds and their cries.

SUDDEN THAW

When day dawned with unusual light,
Hedges in snow stood half their height
And in the white-paved village street
Children were walking without feet.

But now by their own breath kept warm
Muck-heaps are naked at the farm
And even through the shrinking snow
Dead bents and thistles start to grow.

HELEN CRUICKSHANK

SHY GEORDIE

Up the Noran Water,
In by Inglismaddy,
Annie's got a bairnie
That hasna got a daddy.
Some say it's Tammas's
And some say it's Chay's;
An' naebody expec'it it,
Wi' Annie's quiet ways.

Up the Noran Water,
The bonnie little mannie
Is dandlit an' cuddlit close
By Inglismaddy's Annie.
Wha the bairnie's faither is
The lassie never says;
But some think it's Tammas's,
And some think it's Chay's.

Up the Noran Water,
The country folk are kind;
An' wha the bairnie's daddy is
They dinna muckle mind.
But oh! the bairn at Annie's breist,
The love in Annie's e'e'!
They mak' me wish wi' a' my micht
The lucky lad was me!

MARY STUART

My brother Jamie lost me all,
Fell cleverly to make me fall,
And with a sure reluctant hand
Stole my life and took my land.

It was jealousy of the womb
That let me in and shut him out,
Honesty, kingship, all shut out,
While I enjoyed the royal room.

My father was his, but not my mother,
We were, yet were not, sister, brother,
To reach my mother he had to strike
Me down and leap that deadly dyke.

Over the wall I watched him move
At ease through all the guarded grove,
Then hack, and hack, and hack it down,
Until that ruin was his own.

SCOTLAND 1941

We were a tribe, a family, a people.
Wallace and Bruce guard now a painted field,
And all may read the folio of our fable,
Peruse the sword, the sceptre and the shield.
A simple sky roofed in that rustic day,
The busy corn-fields and the haunted holms,
The green road winding up the ferny brae.
But Knox and Melville clapped their preaching palms
And bundled all the harvesters away,
Hoodicrow Peden in the blighted corn
Hacked with his rusty beak the starving haulms.
Out of that desolation we were born.

Courage beyond the point and obdurate pride
Made us a nation, robbed us of a nation.
Defiance absolute and myriad-eyed
That could not pluck the palm plucked our damnation.
We with such courage and the bitter wit
To fell the ancient oak of loyalty,
And strip the peopled hill and the altar bare,
And crush the poet with an iron text,
How could we read our souls and learn to be?
Here a dull drove of faces harsh and vexed,
We watch our cities burning in their pit,
To salve our souls grinding dull lucre out,
We, fanatics of the frustrate and the half,
Who once set Purgatory Hill in doubt.
Now smoke and dearth and money everywhere,
Mean heirlooms of each fainter generation,
And mummied housegods in their musty niches,
Burns and Scott, sham bards of a sham nation,
And spiritual defeat wrapped warm in riches,
No pride but pride of pelf. Long since the young
Fought in great bloody battles to carve out
This towering pulpit of the Golden Calf.
Montrose, Mackail, Argyle, perverse and brave,
Twisted the stream, unhooped the ancestral hill.
Never had Dee or Don or Yarrow or Till
Huddled such thriftless honour in a grave.

Such wasted bravery idle as a song,
Such hard-won ill might prove Time's verdict wrong,
And melt to pity the annalist's iron tongue.

THEN

There were no men and women then at all,
But the flesh lying alone,
And angry shadows fighting on a wall
That now and then sent out a groan
Buried in lime and stone,
And sweated now and then like tortured wood
Big drops that looked yet did not look like blood.

And yet as each drop came a shadow faded
And left the wall.
There was a lull
Until another in its shadow arrayed it,
Came, fought and left a blood-mark on the wall;
And that was all; the blood was all.

If there had been women there they might have wept
For the poor blood, unowned, unwanted,
Blank as forgotten script.
The wall was haunted
By mute maternal presences whose sighing
Fluttered the fighting shadows and shook the wall
As if that fury of death itself were dying.

THE LITTLE GENERAL

Early in spring the little General came
   Across the sound, bringing the island death,
And suddenly a place without a name,
   And like the pious ritual of a faith,

Hunter and quarry in the boundless trap,
   The white smoke curling from the silver gun,
The feather curling in the hunter's cap,
   And clouds of feathers floating in the sun,

While down the birds came in a deafening shower,
   Wing-hurricane, and the cattle fled in fear.
Up on the hill a remnant of a tower
   Had watched that single scene for many a year,

Weaving a wordless tale where all were gathered
   (Hunter and quarry and watcher and fabulous field),
A sylvan war half human and half feathered,
   Perennial emblem painted on the shield

Held up to cow a never-conquered land
Fast in the little General's fragile hand.

43

THE SUFFICIENT PLACE

See, all the silver roads wind in, lead in
To this still place like evening. See, they come
Like messengers bearing gifts to this little house,
And this great hill worn down to a patient mound,
And these tall trees whose motionless branches bear
An aeon's summer foliage, leaves so thick
They seem to have robbed a world of shade, and kept
No room for all these birds that line the boughs
With heavier riches, leaf and bird and leaf.
Within the doorway stand
Two figures, Man and Woman, simple and clear
As a child's first images. Their manners are
Such as were known before the earliest fashion
Taught the Heavens guile. The room inside is like
A thought that needed thus much space to write on,
Thus much, no more. Here all's sufficient. None
That comes complains, and all the world comes here,
Comes, and goes out again, and comes again.
This is the Pattern, these the Archetypes,
Sufficient, strong, and peaceful. All outside
From end to end of the world is tumult. Yet
These roads do not turn in here but writhe on
Round the wild earth for ever. If a man
Should chance to find this place three times in time
His eyes are changed and make a summer silence
Amid the tumult, seeing the roads wind in
To their still home, the house and the leaves and birds.

THE RIVER

The silent stream flows on and in its glass
Shows the trained terrors, the well-practised partings,
The old woman standing at the cottage gate,
Her hand upon her grandson's shoulder. He,
A bundle of clouts creased as with tribulations,
Bristling with spikes and spits and bolts of steel,
Bound in with belts, the rifle's snub-nosed horn

Peering above his shoulder, looks across
From this new world to hers and tries to find
Some ordinary words that share her sorrow.
The stream flows on
And shows a blackened field, a burning wood,
A bridge that stops half-way, a hill split open
With scraps of houses clinging to its sides,
Stones, planks and tiles and chips of glass and china
Strewn on the slope as by a wrecking wave
Among the grass and wild-flowers. Darkness falls,
The stream flows through the city. In its mirror
Great oes and capitals and flourishes,
Pillars and towers and fans and gathered sheaves
Hold harvest-home and Judgment Day of fire.
The houses stir and pluck their roofs and walls
Apart as if in play and fling their stones
Against the sky to make a common arc
And fall again. The conflagrations raise
Their mountainous precipices. Living eyes
Glaze instantly in crystal change. The stream
Runs on into the day of time and Europe,
Past the familiar walls and friendly roads,
Now thronged with dumb migrations, gods and altars
That travel towards no destination. Then
The disciplined soldiers come to conquer nothing,
March upon emptiness and do not know
Why all is dead and life has hidden itself.
The enormous winding frontier walls fall down,
Leaving anonymous stone and vacant grass.
The stream flows on into what land, what peace,
Far past the other side of the burning world?

A BIRTHDAY

I never felt so much
Since I have felt at all
The tingling smell and touch
Of dogrose and sweet briar,
Nettles against the wall,

45

All sours and sweets that grow
Together or apart
In hedge or marsh or ditch.
I gather to my heart
Beast, insect, flower, earth, water, fire,
In absolute desire,
As fifty years ago.

Acceptance, gratitude:
The first look and the last
When all between has passed
Restore ingenuous good
That seeks no personal end,
Nor strives to mar or mend.
Before I touched the food
Sweetness ensnared my tongue;
Before I saw the wood
I loved each nook and bend,
The track going right and wrong;
Before I took the road
Direction ravished my soul.
Now that I can discern
It whole or almost whole,
Acceptance and gratitude
Like travellers return
And stand where first they stood.

SCOTLAND'S WINTER

Now the ice lays its smooth claws on the sill,
The sun looks from the hill
Helmed in his winter casket,
And sweeps his arctic sword across the sky.
The water at the mill
Sounds more hoarse and dull.
The miller's daughter walking by
With frozen fingers soldered to her basket
Seems to be knocking
Upon a hundred leagues of floor

With her light heels, and mocking
Percy and Douglas dead,
And Bruce on his burial bed,
Where he lies white as may
With wars and leprosy,
And all the kings before
This land was kingless,
And all the singers before
This land was songless,
This land that with its dead and living waits the Judgement
    Day.
But they, the powerless dead,
Listening can hear no more
Than a hard tapping on the sounding floor
A little overhead
Of common heels that do not know
Whence they come or where they go
And are content
With their poor frozen life and shallow banishment.

HUGH MACDIARMID (C.M. Grieve)

O JESU PARVULE
'Followis ane sang of the birth of Christ,
with the tune of Baw lu la law.'
THE GUDE AND GODLIE BALLATIS

His mither sings to the bairnie Christ
Wi' the tune o' *Baw lu la law.*
The bonnie wee craturie lauchs in His crib
An' a' the starnies an' he are sib.
    Baw, baw, my loonikie, baw, balloo.

'Fa' owre, my hinny, fa' owre, fa' owre,
A' body's sleepin' binna oorsels.'
She's drawn Him in tae the bool o' her briest
But the byspale's nae thocht o' sleep i' the least.
    Balloo, wee mannie, balloo, balloo.

binna—except   bool—curve

47

THE BONNIE BROUKIT BAIRN

Mars is braw in crammasy,
Venus in a green silk goun,
The auld mune shaks her gowden feathers,
Their starry talk's a wheen o blethers,
Nane for thee a thochtie sparin,
Earth, thou bonnie broukit bairn!
—*But greet, an in your tears ye'll droun*
The haill clanjamfrie!

blethers—nonsense   clanjamfrie—the lot of them

THE EEMIS-STANE

I' the how-dumb-deid o the cauld hairst nicht
The warl like an eemis-stane
Wags i the lift;
An my eerie memories fa'
Like a yowdendrift.

Like a yowdendrift so's I couldna read
The words cut oot i the stane
Had the fug o fame
An history's hazelraw
No' yirdit thaim.

eemis-stane—stone that can be rocked but does not fall   how-dumb-deid—midnight   lift—sky   yowdendrift—swirl of snow   fug—moss   hazelraw—lichen   yirdit—buried

EMPTY VESSEL

I met ayont the cairney
A lass wi tousie hair
Singin till a bairnie
That was nae langer there.

Wunds wi warlds tae swing
Dinna sing sae sweet.
The licht that bends owre aathing
Is less taen up wi't.

cairney—pile of stones   tousie—tousled   licht—light

THE WATERGAW

Ae weet forenicht i the yow-trummle
I saw yon antrin thing,
A watergaw wi its chitterin licht
Ayont the on-ding;
An I thocht o the last wild look ye gied
Afore ye deed!

There was nae reek i the laverock's hoose
That nicht—an nane i mine;
But I hae thocht o that foolish licht
Ever sin syne;
An I think that mebbe at last I ken
What your look meant then.

watergaw—rainbow   forenicht—evening   yow-trummle (ewe tremble)—cold spell after sheep-shearing   antrin—rare   chitterin—shivering   on-ding—downpour

AN APPRENTICE ANGEL
(To L. M. W.)

I
Try on your wings; I ken vera weel
It wadna look seemly if ony ane saw
A Glasgow Divine ga'en flutherin' aboot
In his study like a drunk craw.

But it 'ud look waur if you'd to bide
In an awkward squad for a month or mair
Learnin' to flee afore you could join
Heaven's air gymkhana aince you got there.

Try on your wings, and gi'e a bit flap,
Pot belly and a', what does it maitter?
Seriously prepare for your future state
—Tho' that's never been in your natur'!

II

As the dragonfly's hideous larva creeps
Oot o' the ditch whaur it was spawned
And straight is turned to the splendid fly,
Nae doot by Death's belated hand
You'll be changed in a similar wey,
But as frae that livin' flash o' licht
The cruel features and crawlin' legs
O' its former state never vanish quite
I fancy your Presbyterian Heaven
'Ll be haunted tae wi' a hellish leaven.

O WHA'S BEEN HERE AFORE ME, LASS

O wha's the bride that cairries the bunch
O' thistles blinterin white?
Her cuckold bridegroom little dreids
What he sall ken this nicht.

For closer than gudeman can come
And closer to'r than hersel,
Wha didna need her maidenheid
Has wrocht his purpose fell.

O wha's been here afore me, lass,
And hoo did he get in?
  —A man that deed or I was born
  This evil thing has din.

And left, as it were on a corpse,
Your maidenheid to me?
  —Nae lass, gudeman, sin Time began
  'S hed ony mair to gie.

  But I can gie ye kindness, lad,
  And a pair o willin hands,
  And ye sall hae my briests like stars,
  My limbs like willow wands.

50

And on my lips ye'll heed nae mair,
And in my hair forget,
The seed o a' the men that in
My virgin womb hae met.

MILK-WORT AND BOG-COTTON

Cwa' een like milk-wort and bog-cotton hair!
I love you, earth, in this mood best o a'
When the shy spirit like a laich wind moves
And frae the lift nae shadow can fa'
Since there's nocht left to thraw a shadow there
Owre een like milk-wort and milk-white cotton hair.

Wad that nae leaf upon anither wheeled
A shadow either and nae root need dern
In sacrifice to let sic beauty be!
But deep surroondin darkness I discern
Is aye the price o licht. Wad licht revealed
Naething but you, and nicht nocht else concealed.

cwa'—come away   laich—southerly   dern—hide

LO! A CHILD IS BORN

I thought of a house where the stones seemed suddenly
    changed
And became instinct with hope, hope as solid as themselves,
And the atmosphere warm with that lovely heat,
The warmth of tenderness and longing souls, the smiling
    anxiety
That rules a home where a child is about to be born.
The walls were full of ears. All voices were lowered.
Only the mother had the right to groan or complain.
Then I thought of the whole world. Who cares for its travail
And seeks to encompass it in like lovingkindness and
    peace?
There is a monstrous din of the sterile who contribute
    nothing

To the great end in view, and the future fumbles,
A bad birth, not like the child in that gracious home
Heard in the quietness turning in its mother's womb,
A strategic mind already, seeking the best way
To present himself to life, and at last, resolved,
Springing into history quivering like a fish,
Dropping into the world like a ripe fruit in due time.—
But where is the Past to which Time, smiling through her
   tears
At her new-born son, can turn crying: 'I love you'?

FROM SECOND HYMN TO LENIN

Oh, it's nonsense, nonsense,
Nonsense at this time o' day
That breid-and-butter problems
S'ud be in ony man's way.

They s'ud be like the tails we tint
On leaving the monkey stage;
A' maist folk fash aboot's alike
Primaeval to oor age.

We're grown-up folk that haena yet
Put bairnly things aside
—A' that's material and moral—
And oor new state descried.

Sport, love, and parentage,
Trade, politics, and law
S'ud be nae mair to us than braith
We hardly ken we draw.

Freein' oor poo'ers for greater things,
And feg's there's plenty o' them,
Tho' wha's still trammelt in alow
Canna be tenty o' them.

fash—bother   tenty—aware

WITH THE HERRING FISHERS

'I see herrin'.'—I hear the glad cry
And 'gainst the moon see ilka blue jowl
In turn as the fishermen haul on the nets
And sing: 'Come, shove in your heids and growl.'

'Soom on, bonnie herrin', soom on,' they shout,
Or 'Come in, O come in, and see me,'
'Come gie the auld man something to dae.
It'll be a braw change frae the sea.'

O it's ane o' the bonniest sichts in the warld
To watch the herrin' come walkin' on board
In the wee sma' 'oors o' a simmer's mornin'
As if o' their ain accord.

For this is the way that God sees life,
The haill jing-bang o's appearin
Up owre frae the edge o' naethingness
It's his happy cries I'm hearin'.

'Left, right—O come in and see me,'
Reid and yellow and black and white
Toddlin' up into Heaven thegither
At peep o' day frae the endless night.

'I see herrin',' I hear his glad cry,
And 'gainst the moon see his muckle blue jowl,
As he handles buoy-tow and bush raip
Singin': 'Come, shove in your heids and growl!'

soom—swim   jing-bang—mob   toddlin'—walking with small steps
muckle—big   bush raip—bush-rope

TWO MEMORIES

Religion? Huh! Whenever I hear the word
It brings two memories back to my mind.
Choose between them, and tell me which
You think the better model for mankind.

Fresh blood scares sleeping cows worse than anything on
  earth.
An unseen rider leans far out from his horse with a
  freshly-skinned
Weaner's hide in his hands, turning and twisting the hairy
  slimy thing
And throwing the blood abroad on the wind.

A brilliant flash of lightning crashes into the heavens.
It reveals the earth in a strange yellow-green light,
Alluring yet repelling, that distorts the immediate
  foreground
And makes the grey and remote distance odious to the
  sight.

And a great mass of wraithlike objects on the bed ground
Seems to upheave, to move, to rise, to fold and undulate
In a wavelike mobility that extends to an alarming distance.
The cows have ceased to rest; they are getting to their feet.

Another flash of lightning shows a fantastic and fearsome
  vision.
Like the branches of some enormous grotesque sprawling
  plant
A forest of long horns waves, and countless faces
Turn into the air, unspeakably weird and gaunt.
The stroke of white fire from the sky is reflected back
To the heavens from thousands of bulging eyeballs,
And into the heart of any man who sees
This diabolical mirroring of the lightning numbing fear
  falls.

Is such a stampede your ideal for the human race?
Haven't we milled in it long enough? My second memory
Is of a flight of wild swans. Glorious white birds in the
  blue October heights
Over the surly unrest of the ocean! Their passing is more
  than music to me
And from their wings descends, and in my heart
  triumphantly peals,
The old loveliness of Earth that both affirms and heals.

FROM THE GLASS OF PURE WATER

Hold a glass of pure water to the eye of the sun!
It is difficult to tell the one from the other
Save by the tiny hardly visible trembling of the water.
This is the nearest analogy to the essence of human life
Which is even more difficult to see.
Dismiss anything you can see more easily;
It is not alive—it is not worth seeing.
There is a minute indescribable difference
Between one glass of pure water and another
With slightly different chemical constituents.
The difference between one human life and another
Is no greater; colour does not colour the water:
You cannot tell a white man's life from a black man's.
But the lives of these particular slum people
I am chiefly concerned with, like the lives of all
The world's poorest, remind me less
Of a glass of water held between my eyes and the sun
—They remind me of the feeling they had
Who saw Sacco and Vanzetti in the death cell
On the eve of their execution.
—One is talking to God.

I dreamt last night that I saw one of His angels
Making his centennial report to the Recording Angel
On the condition of human life.
Look at the ridge of skin between your thumb and
    forefinger.
Look at the delicate lines on it and how they change
—How many different things they can express—
As you move out or close in your forefinger and thumb.
And look at the changing shapes—the countless
Little gestures, little miracles of line—
Of your forefinger and thumb as you move them.
And remember how much a hand can express,
How a single slight movement of it can say more
Than millions of words—dropped hand, clenched fist,
Snapping fingers, thumb up, thumb down,
Raised in blessing, clutched in passion, begging,

Welcome, dismissal, prayer, applause,
And a million other signs, too slight, too subtle,
Too packed with meaning for words to describe,
A universal language understood by all.
And the Angel's report on human life
Was the subtlest movement—just like that—and no more;
A hundred years of life on the Earth
Summed up, not a detail missed or wrongly assessed,
In that little inconceivably intricate movement.

The only communication between man and man
That says anything worth hearing
—The hidden well-water; the finger of destiny—
Moves as that water, that angel, moved.
Truth is the rarest thing and life
The gentlest, most unobtrusive movement in the world.
I cannot speak to you of the poor people of all the world
But among the people in these nearest slums I know
This infinitesimal twinkling, this delicate play
Of tiny signs that not only say more

Than all speech, but all there is to say,
All there is to say and to know and to be.
There alone I seldom find anything else,
Each in himself or herself a dramatic whole,
An 'agon' whose validity is timeless.

Our duty is to free that water, to make these gestures,
To help humanity to shed all else,
All that stands between any life and the sun,
The quintessence of any life and the sun;
To still all sound save that talking to God . . .

WILLIAM JEFFREY

STONES

The stones in Jordan's stream
Perceived the dove descend
In its lily of light;

56

That glory entered
Their interminable dream.

The stones in Edom's wilderness
Observed the fiend
Take five of their number
And build a cairn thereof,
And beckoning to Jesus
He pointed to the stones and said:
'Make bread.'
But because of His great love
For the uniqueness of created things,
The confraternity in disparity
Of plant and rock, of flesh and wings,
Jesus would not translate the stones
Out of their immobile immortality
Into that dynasty of death,
Decaying bread;
And the stones were gratified
And shone underneath his tread.

The stones upon Golgotha's hill
Took the shadow of the Cross
Upon them like the scorch of ice;
And they felt the flick of dice
And Jesus' blood mingling with His mother's tears;
And these made indelible stains,
And some of them were taken up
And with curses thrown
At that rejected Throne,
And others felt the clamorous butts of Roman spears:
And the pity, horror, and love within them pent
Welled out and shook the earth.
And the veil was rent.
The great stones of the tomb
Enfolded Jesus' body
In silence and deep gloom.
They had Him to themselves alone,
That shard of Him, sinew and bone,
Transient dust on their immortality.

And now their inanimate heart
Yearned over that shrouded form:
And while three midnights passed
They made of that tomb
A womb:
The fragile bones renewed their strength,
The flesh trembled and moved,
The glory of the dove
Re-descended from above,
And with the break of day
The door was rolled away:
The function of the stones was done:
His second birth
Achieved on earth,
Jesus walked into the sun.

NATIVE ELEMENT

A cloud walking.
                    Thus a child had said
Watching the landward progress of a swan
Emerge in drip of silver from a pond,
Questing sweet roots and grasses succulent.

And as the bird advanced with serpent head
Elatedly he seemed to entertain
The self-same thought. But almost instantly
His cumber'd carriage and his weighted bones
Dissuaded him. A thousand ages bent
Their arc on him. The brontosaurus moved
In his deliberate web-footed gait:
He was the essence of ungainliness.

Returned now. Oxen-wise in reeds he knelt,
And thrusting forth the snowdrift of his breast
Upon the silver water fell to rest,
At one again with his own element.

Now all the lissomness of wind and wave
Was gathered in his beauty and his pride,

No hint of any clumsiness was there,
But all was poised to perfect functioning.
He paused, and shook the glory of each wing,
And then in stillness glided on, within
His sky the sole majestic Jupiter.

DONALD SINCLAIR

SLIGH NAN SEANN SEUN

Saoibhir sith nan sian an nochd air Tìr-an-Àigh.
Is ciùine ciùil nam fiath ag iadhadh Innse Gràidh,
Is èasgaidh gach sgiath air fianlach dian ad Dàin
Is slighe nan seann seun a' siaradh siar gun tàmh.
Saoibhir com nan cruach le cuimhne làithean aosd',
Sona gnùis nan cuan am bruadair uair a dh'aom;
Soillseach gach uair an aigne suaimhneach ghaoth—
O, làithean mo luaidh, 'ur n—uaill, 'ur n-uails', 'ur gaol!
O, làithean geala gràidh le'r gnàthan geala còir,
O, aimsirean an àigh le'r gàire, gean, is ceòl—
O, shaoghail nan gràs nan gathan aithne 's eoil,
C'uime thréig 's nach d'fhàg ach àilte àin 'ur glòir?
An ioghnadh deòin is dùil bhi dol an null 'nur déidh,
Ri ionndruinn nan rùn a lìon 'ur sgùird le spéis?
An ioghnadh ceòl nan dùl bhi seinn air cliù 'ur réim'
Is fabhra crom gach sùl bhi tais fo dhùbhradh leug?
A làithean sin a thriall le ial-luchd àis mo shluaigh,
C'uime thàrr 'ur miann gach dias a b'fhiachmhor buaidh?
An ioghnadh an iarmailt shiar bhi nochd fo shnuadh,
'S 'ur n-àrosan an cian bhi laist le lias bith-bhuan?
An ioghnadh lom gach làir bhi luaidh air làn 'ur sgeòil?
An ioghnadh cnuic is ràdh a' chomha-thràth 'nam beòil?
An ioghnadh cruit nan dàn bhi bìth fo sgàil' a neòil—
Is ealaidh-ghuth nam bàrd gun seun, gun sàire seòil?
Chan ioghnadh cill mo shluaigh an cois nan cuan bhi balbh,
Chan ioghnadh uchd nan tuam bhi'n tòic le luach na
    dh'fhalbh,
O, shaoghail, is truagh nach till aon uair a shearg,
'S nach tàrr mo dheòin, ge buan, aon fhios á suain nam
    marbh!

59

THE PATH OF THE OLD SPELLS
from the Gaelic of Donald Sinclair
(Scots version by Hugh MacDiarmid)

Rich is the peace o' the elements the nicht owre the Land
o' Joy
And rich the evenness o' the calm's music roond the Isles
o' Love,
Ilka wing plies urgently in obedience to nature
While the path o' the auld spells winds inexorably
westwards.
Rich the breist o' the hills wi' memories o' bygone days,
Serene the face o' the seas wi' dreams o' the times that
are gane.
O seilfu' days, your pride, your nobleness, you love!
O white days o' love wi' your clean and kindly ways!
O times o' joy wi' your lauchter, your cheer, and your
music!
O warld o' grace, lit by rays o' knowledge and art!
Why ha'e you gane and left hardly a trace o' the noontide
o' your glory?
Is it a wonder desire and hope seek to follow eftir you,
Fain for the secret that aince cled your lap wi' esteem?
Is it a wonder the elements sing o' your time and poo'er
And the curved lid o' ilka eye is weak frae the fire o' jewels?
O yon days that ha'e gane wi' the shinin' load o' the
wisdom o' my race,
Why did you want to strip awa' ilka last ear o' maist
worthy excellence?
Nae wonder the western lift is noo sae illustrious wi' licht
And that yon dwellin's in the distance are alowe wi' an
everlasting flame!
Nae wonder the bareness o' ilka flat bespeaks the fullness
o' your story!
Nae wonder the hills haud the words o' twilicht in their
mooths!
Nae wonder the harp o' the sangs is silent under the belly
o' yon clood
And the voice-of-song o' the bards without spell or
excellence o' art!
Nae wonder the kirkyaird o' my folk, by the sea, is dumb!

Nae wonder the breists o' the graves are a' hoven wi' the
    worth o' what's gane!
O Warld! It is a woe that no' an 'oor that has gane can
    ever come back,
Nor can my desire, tho' lastin', draw a single word frae
    the sleep o' the deid!

MARGOT ROBERT ADAMSON

EDINBURGH

If they should ask what makes the stuff of us
We should call up such idle things and gone!
The theatre we knew in Grindley Street,
The midnight bell vibrating in the Tron.

A church tower's clock along the Lothian Road,
Whose face lit up would turn a lemon moon,
Seen o'er the pallid bleakness of the street
In the chill dusks that harry northern June,

A Sunday morning over Samson's Ribs,
The smoky grass that grows on Arthur's Seat;
Turned-yellow willow leaves in Dalkeith Road,
Dropt lanceheads on the pavement at our feet;

Glimpses got sometimes of the Forfar hills
With the white snows upon them, or, maybe,
Green waters washing round the piers of Leith
With all the straws and flotsam of the sea.

A certain railway bridge whence one can look
On a network of bright lines and feel the stress,
Tossing its plumes of milky snow, where goes
Loud in full pace the thundering North Express.

Behind its great green engine; or in Spring
Black-heaved the Castle Rock and there where blows
By Gordon's window wild the wallflower still,
The gold that keeps the footprints of Montrose.

61

The Pentlands over yellow stubble fields
Seen out beyond Craigmillar, and the flight
Of seagulls wheeling round the dark-shared plough,
Strewing the landscape with a rush of white.

Such idle things! Gold birches by hill lochs,
The gales that beat the Lothian shores in strife,
The day you found the great blue alkanette,
And all the farmlands by the shores of Fife.

WILIAM SOUTAR

THE PHILOSOPHIC TAED

There was a taed wha thocht sae lang
On sanctity and sin;
On what was richt, and what was wrang,
And what was in atween—
That he gat naething düne.

The wind micht blaw, the snaw micht snaw,
He didna mind a wheet;
Nor kent the derk'nin frae the daw,
The wulfire frae the weet;
Nor fuggage frae his feet.

His wife and weans frae time to time,
As they gaed by the cratur,
Wud haut to hae a gowk at him
And shak their pows, or natter:
'He's no like growin better.'

It maun be twenty year or mair
Sin thocht's been a' his trade:
And naebody can tell for shair
Whether this unco taed
Is dead, or thinks he's dead.

THE GOWK

Half doun the hill, whaur fa's the linn
Far frae the flaught o' fowk,
I saw upon a lanely whin
A lanely singin' gowk:
Cuckoo, cuckoo;
And at my back
The howie hill stüde up and spak:
Cuckoo, cuckoo.

There was nae soun': the loupin' linn
Hung frostit in its fa':
Nae bird was on the lanely whin
Sae white wi' fleurs o' snaw:
Cuckoo, cuckoo;
I stüde stane still;
And saftly spak the howie hill:
Cuckoo, cuckoo.

flaught—rush   howie—hollow

THE TRYST

O luely, luely, cam she in
And luely she lay doun:
I kent her be her caller lips
And her breists sae sma' and roun'.

A' thru the nicht we spak nae word
Nor sinder'd bane frae bane:
A' thru the nicht I heard her hert
Gang soundin' wi' my ain.

It was about the waukrife hour
When cocks begin to craw
That she smool'd saftly thru the mirk
Afore the day wud daw.

Sae luely, luely, cam she in
Sae luely was she gaen;
And wi' her a' my simmer days
Like they had never been.

luely—softly   sinder—to part   waukrife—wakeful   smool—to slip
away   mirk—darkness   daw—dawn

THE THOCHT

Young Janie was a strappan lass
Wha deed in jizzen-bed;
And monie a thocht her lover thocht
Lang eftir she was dead:

But aye, wi' a' he brocht to mind
O' misery and wrang,
There was a gledness gether'd in
Like the owrecome o' a sang:

And, gin the deid are naethingness
Or they be minded on,
As hinny to a hungry ghaist
Maun be a thocht like yon.

jizzen-bed—childbirth

THE LANELY MÜNE

Saftly, saftly, through the mirk
The müne walks a' hersel':
Ayont the brae; abüne the kirk;
And owre the dunnlin bell.
I wudna be the müne at nicht
For a' her gowd and a' her licht.

SONG

Whaur yon broken brig hings owre;
Whaur yon water maks nae soun';

Babylon blaws by in stour:
Gang doun wi' a sang, gang doun.

Deep, owre deep, for onie drouth:
Wan eneuch an ye wud droun:
Saut, or seelfu', for the mouth;
Gang doun wi' a sang, gang doun.

Babylon blaws by in stour
Whaur yon water maks nae soun':
Darkness is your only door;
Gang doun wi' a sang, gang doun.

MIRACLE

Summer
Is on the hill;
But in the moveless air
The fountain of the hawthorn hangs
With frost.

REVELATION

Machines of death from east to west
Drone through the darkened sky:
Machines of death from west to east
Through the same darkness fly.

They pass; and on the foredoomed towns
Loosen their slaughtering load:
They see no faces in the stones:
They hear no cries of blood.

They leave a ruin; and they meet
A ruin on return:
The mourners in the alien street
At their own doorways mourn.

THE CHILDREN

Upon the street they lie
Beside the broken stone:
The blood of children stares from the broken stone.

Death came out of the sky
In the bright afternoon:
Darkness slanted over the bright afternoon.

Again the sky is clear
But upon earth a stain:
The earth is darkened with a darkening stain:

A wound which everywhere
Corrupts the hearts of men:
The blood of children corrupts the hearts of men.

Silence is in the air:
The stars move to their places:
Silent and serene the stars move to their places:

But from earth the children stare
With blind and fearful faces:
And our charity is in the children's faces.

MURIEL STUART

THE SEED SHOP

Here in a quiet and dusty room they lie,
    Faded as crumbled stone or shifting sand,
Forlorn as ashes, shrivelled, scentless, dry,
    Meadows and gardens running through my hand.

Dead that shall quicken at the trump of Spring,
    Sleepers to stir beneath June's splendid kiss,
Though birds pass over, unremembering,
    And no bee seek here roses that were his.

In this brown husk a dale of hawthorn dreams,
    A cedar in this narrow cell is thrust
That will drink deeply of a century's streams;
    These lilies shall make Summer on my dust.

Here in their safe and simple house of death,
　　Sealed in their shells a million roses leap;
Here I can blow a garden with my breath,
　　And in my hand a forest lies asleep.

IN THE ORCHARD

'I thought you loved me.'
　　　　　　　　　　　'No, it was only fun.'
'When we stood there, closer than all?'
　　　　　　　　　　　　　　　'Well, the harvest moon
Was shining and queer in your hair, and it turned my head.'
'That made you?'
　　　　　'Yes.'
　　　　　　　　'Just the moon and the light it made
Under the tree?'
　　　　　'Well, your mouth too.'
　　　　　　　　　　　　　　'Yes. My mouth?'
'And the quiet there that sang like the drum in the booth.
You shouldn't have danced like that.'
　　　　　　　　　　　　'Like what?'
　　　　　　　　　　　　　　　　'So close,
With your head turned up, and the flower in your hair, a rose
That smelt all warm.'
　　　　　　　　'I loved you. I thought you knew
I wouldn't have danced like that with any but you.'
'I didn't know. I thought you knew it was fun.'
'I thought it was love you meant.'
　　　　　　　　　　　　'Well, it's done.'
　　　　　　　　　　　　　　　'Yes, it's done
I've seen boys stone a blackbird, and watched them drown
A kitten ... it clawed at the reeds, and they pushed it down
Into the pool while it screamed. Is that fun, too?'
'Well, boys like that . . . your brothers . . .'
　　　　　　　　　　　　　　　'Yes, I know.
But you, so lovely and strong! Not you! Not you!'
'They don't understand it's cruel. It's only a game.'
'And are girls fun, too?'
　　　　　　　　　'No. Still in a way it's the same.
It's queer and lovely to have a girl . . .'
　　　　　　　　　　　　　　'Go on.'
'It makes you mad for a bit to feel she's your own,
And you laugh and kiss her, and maybe you give her a ring,

67

But it's only in fun.'
                              'But I gave you everything.'
'Well, you shouldn't have done it. You know what a
   fellow thinks
When a girl does that.'
                              'Yes, talks of her over his drinks
And calls her a—'
                              'Stop that now. I thought you knew.'
'But it wasn't with anyone else. It was only you.'
'How did I know? I thought you wanted it too.
I thought you were like the rest—Well, what's to be done?'
'To be done?'
                  'Is it all right?'
                                    'Yes.'
                                          'Sure?'
                                                'Yes, but why?'
'I don't know. I thought you were going to cry.
You said you had something to tell me.'
                                          'Yes, I know.
It wasn't anything really . . . I think I'll go.'
'Yes, it's late. There's thunder about, a drop of rain
Fell on my hand in the dark. I'll see you again
At the dance next week. You're sure that everything's
   right?'
'Yes.'
      'Well, I'll be going.'
                              'Kiss me...'
                                          'Good night...'
                                                'Good night.'

ENOUGH

Did he forget? . . . I do not remember,
All I had of him once I still have to-day;
He was lovely to me as the word "amber",
As the taste of honey and as the smell of hay.

What if he forget if I remember?
What more of love have you than I to say?
I have and hold him still in the word "amber",
Taste of honey brings him, he comes back with the hay.

68

HAMISH MACLAREN

ISLAND ROSE

She has given all her beauty to the water;
    She has told her secrets to the tidal bell;
And her hair is a moon-drawn net, and it has caught her,
    And her voice is in the hollow shell.

She will not come back any more now, nor waken
    Out of her island dream where no wind blows:
And only in the small house of the shell, forsaken,
    Sings the dark one whose face is a rose.

ADAM DRINAN (Joseph MacLeod)

SUCCESSFUL SCOT

Gold pins and pearls of Columbia,
    how gross they grow by your drive,
studding an English summer
    with the back-end of your life,
        beknighted and pompous Scot!

By adding figure to figure
    you have developed never,
you have just grown bigger and bigger
    like this wee wort from the heather;
        and size is all you have got.

Your mind set toward London,
    your belly pushing to success,
from the very day that you won
    the Bursary of the West,
        have flagged and faltered not.

Not much has your face altered!
    The man has the mouth of the child.
The Position you planted and watered
    expands from the lad's desires
        as if bound in a pot.

69

And would you return (for the fishing)
   to your island of humbler hours,
there in your tailored wishes
    you would trample your youth in this flower
      that you have forgotten:

Or spending a stay-at-home summer,
   you will never know what they suffer,
these bloated flowers of Columbia;
    you will own the youth of others,
      and never know what.

FROM THE MEN ON THE ROCKS

Our pastures are bitten and bare
our wool is blown to the winds
our mouths are stopped and dumb
our oatfields weak and thin.
Nobody fishes the loch
nobody stalks the deer.
Let us go down to the sea.
The friendly sea likes to be visited.

Our fathers sleep in the cemetery
their boats, cracked, by their side.
The sea turns round in his sleep
pleasurecraft nod on the tide.
Sea ducks slumber on waves
sea eagles have flown away.
Let us put out to sea.
The fat sea likes to be visited.

Fat sea, what's on your shelf?
all the grey night we wrestled.

To muscle, to skill, to petrol,
Hook oo rin yo! . . . one herring!
and of that only the head.
Dogfishes had the rest,
a parting gift from the sea.
The merry waves like to be visited.

Merry sea, what have you sent us?
A rusty English trawler?
The crew put into the hotel
the engineer overhauls her.
Gulls snatch offal to leeward.
We on the jetty await
gifts of the cod we can't afford.
The free sea likes to be visited.

Free were our father's boats
whose guts were strewn on the shore.
Steam ships were bought by the rich
cheap from the last war.
They tear our nets to pieces
and the sea gives them our fishes.
Even he favours the rich.
The false sea likes to be visited.

FROM THE GHOSTS OF THE STRATH

Long blue shadow of salmon lying,
    shot shell of leaping silver,
using the lull and the flies
    to practise for the rough river,
stay down on the salt sea stones,
    learn there, you yet-free fishes.
Your sweet hope to come home
    was once on the hillside fishers.

Salmon may leap falls;
   we deeps of the linn may master:
but weeds grow up our walls,
   hearts whip in airy water.
Up in the rich meads
   such the rich men's power is,
only wrens are safe in streams
   and sheep in houses.

The great power had its magic!
   with strong spells of paper
money and law raised lairds;
   burnt crops bewitched labour.
No cunning of fish-lore
   will conjure our safe return;
but the same black arts be ours—
   from the need to burn, to the burning.

MEASURES

Three measures of breadth I take
that the heart, the hand, and the foot make:
   the candid inches between the eyes of confidence,
   the width of a gull's back in the hand that shot it,
   and the stretch of a water that cannot be walked upon.

And three measures of slenderness I put to these,
in which the eye, the ear, and the mind meet:
   the slimness of a boy's ankle while he is alive to dance,
   the whisper that draws a hill across a strath,
   and that which separates self-respect from self-regard.

ELEGY
(for William Soutar)

A narrowing of knowledge to one window to a door
Swinging inward on a man in a windless room
On a man inwardly singing
                              on a singing child
Alone and never alone a lonely child
Singing
          in a mirror dancing to a dancing child
Memory sang and words in a mimic dance
Old words were young and a child sang.

A narrowing of knowledge to one room to a doorway
To a door in a wall swinging bringing him friends
A narrowing of knowledge to
                              an arrow in bone in the marrow
An arrow
          death
                    strung on the string of the spine.

To the live crystal in the palm and the five fingers
To the slow thirty years' pearl in the hand
Shelled in a skull in the live face of a statue
Sea-flowered on the neck of broken marble
Sunken fourteen years in that aquarium.

ALBERT D. MACKIE

MOLECATCHER

Strampin' the bent, like the Angel o' Daith,
    The mowdie-man staves by;
Alang his pad the mowdie-worps
    Like sma' Assyrians lie.

And where the Angel o' Daith has been,
    Yirked oot o' their yirdy hames,
Lie Sennacherib's blasted hosts
    Wi' guts dung oot o' wames.

73

Sma' black tramorts wi' gruntles grey,
    Sma' weak weemin's han's,
Sma' bead-een that wid touch ilk hert
    Binnae the mowdie-man's.

yirked—jerked   yirdy—earthy

NEWSBOY

I heard a puir deleerit loon
    Cryan papers through the nicht
       Wi deil a sowl to buy.
       Me aa owre, thinks I,
    Singan sangs wi aa my micht
And nane to hear a sound.

ROBERT MACLELLAN

SANG

There's a reid lowe in yer cheek,
Mither, and a licht in yer ee,
And ye sing like the shuilfie in the slae,
But no for me.

The man that cam the day,
Mither, that ye ran to meet,
He drapt his gun and fondlet ye
And I was left to greit.

Ye served him kail frae the pat,
Mither, and meat frae the bane.
Ye brocht him cherries frae the gean,
And I gat haurdly ane.

And nou he lies in yer bed,
Mither, and the licht growes dim,
And the sang ye sing as ye hap me ower
Is meant for him.

74

Robert Garioch

SISYPHUS

Bumpity doun in the corrie gaed whuddran the pitiless
  whun stane.
Sisyphus, pechan and sweitan, disjaskit, forfeuchan and
  broun'd-aff,
sat on the heather a hanlawhile, houpan the Boss didna
  spy him,
seean the terms of his contract includit nae mention of
  tea-breaks,
syne at the muckle big scunnersome boulder he trauchlit
  aince mair,
Ach, hou kenspeckle it was, that he ken'd ilka spreckle
  and blotch on't.
Heavan awa at its wecht, he manhaunnlit the bruitt up
  the brae-face,
takkan the easiest gait he had fand in a fudder of dour
  years,
hauddan awa frae the craigs had affrichtit him maist in
  his youth-heid,
feelan his years aa the same, he gaed cannily, tenty of
  slipped discs.
Eftir an hour and a quarter he warslit his wey to the
  brae's heid,
hystit his boulder richt up on the tap of the cairn—and it
  stude there!
streikit his length on the chuckie-stanes, houpan the Boss
  wadna spy him,

corrie—mountain hollow   gaed whuddran—went rushing   whun
stane—whinstone   pechan—panting   sweitan—sweating   disjaskit—
worn out   forfeuchan—exhausted   broun'd-aff—browned-off
hanlawhile—short time   syne—then   scunnersome—disgusting
trauchlit—struggled   aince mair—once more   kenspeckle—well-
known   spreckle—speckle   on't—on it   wecht—weight   bruitt—
brute   brae—slope   gait—way   fand—found   fudder—large
number   dour—hard   craigs—rocks   affrichtit—frightened
maist—most   gaed cannily—went carefully   tenty—wary   warslit—
struggled   streikit—stretched   chuckie-stanes—pebblestones

75

had a wee look at the scenery, feenisht a pie and a cheese-
    piece.
Whit was he thinkan about, that he jist gied the boulder a
    wee shove?
Bumpity doun in the corrie gaed whuddran the pitiless
    whun stane,
Sisyphus dodderan eftir it, shair of his cheque at the
    month's end.

gied—gave   dodderan—toddling   shair—sure

ELEGY (Edinburgh Sonnet 16)

They are lang deid, folk that I used to ken,
their firm-set lips aa mowdert and agley,
sherp-tempert een rusty amang the cley:
they are baith deid, thae wycelike, bienlie men,

heidmaisters, that had been in pouer for ten
or twenty year afore fate's taiglit wey
brocht me, a young, weill-harnit, blate and fey
new-cleckit dominie, intill their den.

Ane tellt me it was time I learnt to write—
round-haund, he meant—and saw about my hair:
I mind of him, beld-heidit, wi a kyte.

Ane sneerit quarterly—I cuidna square
my savings-bank—and sniftert in his spite.
Weill, gin they arena deid, it's time they were.

BRITHER WORM

I saw a lang worm snoove throu the space atween twa
    stanes,
pokan its heid, if it had ane, up throu a hole in the New
    Toun,

up throu a crack ye wad hardly hae seen in an area of stane,
unkenn'd upliftit tons of mason-wark piled on the soil,
wi causey-streets, biggit of granite setts, like blank waas
    flat on the grund,
plainstane pavements of Thurso slabs laid owre the stane-
    aircht cellars,
the area fifteen feet doun, wi weill-fittan flagstanes,
    Regency wark.
Nou, in my deedit stane-and-lime property awntert a nesh
    and perfect worm,
and I was abasit wi thochts of what was gaun-on ablow
    my feet,
that the feu'd and rentit grund was the soil of the
    Drumsheuch Forest,
and that life gaed on inunder the grund-waa-stane and
    had sent out a spy,
jalousan some Frien of the Worms had brocht a maist
    welcome shoure,
whan I on my side of the crust had teemit a pail of water,
meaning to gie the place a guid scrub-doun wi a stable-
    besom.
Sae a lang, saft, sappy and delicate pink and naukit cratur
neatly wan out frae atween thae weil-fittan chiselled,
    unnaitural stanes.
I watched and thocht lang of the wonders of Nature, and
    didna muve,
and thocht of the deeps of the soil, deeper nor the sea,
    and I made nae sound.
A rat raxt frae a crack atween twa stanes.
My hale body sheuk wi the grue.
It keekit at me, and was gane.

---

snoove—glide   unkenn'd—unknown   causey-streets—cobbled streets
biggit—built   stane-aircht—stone-arched   awntert—adventured
nesh—delicate   gaun-on—going on   grund-waa-stane—central stone
jalousan—guessing   brocht—brought   shoure—shower   teemit—
emptied   guid—good   besom—broom   naukit—naked   nor—
than   raxt—stretched   grue—shudder   keekit—peeped

NEMO CANEM IMPUNE LACESSIT

I kicked an Edinbro dug-luver's dug,
leastways, I tried: my timing wes owre late.
It stopped whit it wes daein on my gate
and skelpit aff to find some ither mug.

Whit a sensation! If a clockwark thug
suid croun ye wi a brolly owre yir pate,
the Embro folk wad leave ye to yir fate;
it's you, maist like, wad get a flee in yir lug.

But kick the Friend of Man! Or hae a try!
The Friend of Wummin, even, that's far waur
a felony, mair dangerous, forby.

Meddle wi puir dumb craiturs gin ye daur.
That maks ye a richt cruel bruitt, my! my!
And whit d'ye think yir braw front gate is for?

AND THEY WERE RICHT

I went to see 'Ane Tryall of Heretiks'
by Fionn MacColla, treatit as a play;
a wycelike wark, but what I want to say
is mair taen-up wi halie politics

nor wi the piece itsel; the kinna tricks
the unco-guid get up til when they hae
their wey. Yon late-nicht plöy on Setturday
was thrang wi Protestants and Catholics,

an eydent audience, wi fowth of bricht
arguments wad hae kept them gaun till Monday.
It seemed discussion wad last out the nicht,

78

hadna the poliss, sent by Mrs Grundy
pitten us out at twalve. And they were richt!
Wha daur debait religion on a Sunday?

PROEM AND INSCRIPTION FOR A HERMES

Heat, and a dazzle of brichtness,
        and white-het stuir on the pathway;
lang is the gait I hae traipst,
        monie a mile I maun gae.
Ach! but I'm drouthie and weary
        of lime-dry roads, and the Sun's rays
ding on my untheikit heid;
        het are my harns and my taes.
Aye, and it's queer that the malice
        of deid things gies us sic sad pain:
what is ma heid to the Sun?
        what are ma feet to the stanes?
Hou can I haud to ma life on the dreich deid yird,
        or the green grain
growe in the dessicat marl,
        whaur sunlicht allanerlie reigns?
Sudden I riddle the answer,
        the guid news carved on a reuch stane,
phallic in form, and erect,
        staunds by the road as I gae;
livan, a stane wi a voice
        that is cut deep intill the lime grain:
Hermes the God, it is he
        that greets me and shaws me the way:

'Hermes I am; here I bide,
        whaur the saft souchs whish in the lime trees,

marking the airts of the cross-roads,
near the glittering sea.
Wearyit traivlers, I offer ye cool shade,
bieldin for hairt's ease,
caller and colourless spring water
that bubbles out free.'

GEORGE BRUCE

INHERITANCE

This which I write now
Was written years ago
Before my birth
In the features of my father.

It was stamped
In the rock formations
West of my hometown.
Not I write,

But, perhaps, William Bruce,
Cooper.
Perhaps here his hand
Well articled in his trade.

Then though my words
Hit out
An ebullition from
City or flower,

There not my faith,
These the paint
Smeared upon
The inarticulate,

The salt crusted sea-boot,
The red-eyed mackerel,
The plate shining with herring,
And many men,

Seamen and craftsmen and curers,
And behind them
The protest of hundreds of years,
The sea obstinate against the land.

KINNAIRD HEAD

I go North to cold, to home, to Kinnaird,
Fit monument for our time.

This is the outermost edge of Buchan.
Inland the sea birds range,
The tree's leaf has salt upon it,
The tree turns to the low stone wall.
And here a promontory rises towards Norway,
Irregular to the top of thin grey grass
Where the spindrift in storm lays its beads.
The water plugs in the cliff sides,
The gull cries from the clouds
This is the consummation of the plain.

O impregnable and very ancient rock,
Rejecting the violence of water,
Ignoring its accumulations and strategy,
You yield to history nothing.

THE FISHERMAN

As he comes from one of those small houses
Set within the curve of the low cliff
For a moment he pauses
Foot on step at the low lintel
Before fronting wind and sun.
He carries out from within something of the dark
Concealed by heavy curtain,
Or held within the ship under hatches.

Yet with what assurance
The compact body moves,
Head pressed to wind,
His being at an angle
As to anticipate the lurch of earth.

Who is he to contain night
And still walk stubborn
Holding the ground with light feet
And with a careless gait?
Perhaps a cataract of light floods,
Perhaps the apostolic flame.
Whatever it may be
The road takes him from us.
Now the pier is his, now the tide.

TOM ON THE BEACH

With bent back, world's curve on it,
I brood over my pretty pool
And hunt the pale, flat, sand-coloured
Fish, with cupped hands, in the cold.
Ah, but my warm heart, with hope
Wrapped in it in the bright afternoon
Feet glittering in the sand,
Eyes on my pale prey, was sure.

Suns have passed, suns have passed,
Skies purple above the thin sand.
With bent back brooding on the round
World, over my shoulder

I feel the touch of a future
In the cold. The little fish
Come not near me, cleaving
To their element and flattening on the sand.

How many years since with sure heart
And prophecy of success
Warmed in it
Did I look with delight on the little fish,

Start with happiness, the warm sun on me?
Now the waters spread horizonwards,
Great skies meet them,
I brood upon uncompleted tasks.

A GATEWAY TO THE SEA (I)
At the East Port, St Andrews

Pause stranger at the porch: nothing beyond
This framing arch of stone, but scattered rocks
And sea and these on the low beach
Original to the cataclysm and the dark.

Once one man bent to the stone, another
Dropped the measuring line, a third and fourth
Together lifted and positioned the dressed stone
Making wall and arch; yet others
Settled the iron doors on squawking hinge
To shut without the querulous seas and men.
Order and virtue and love (they say)
Dwelt in the town—but that was long ago.
Then the stranger at the gate, the merchants,
Missioners, the blind beggar with the dog,
The miscellaneous vendors (duly inspected)
Were welcome within the wall that held from sight
The water's brawl. All that was long ago.
Now the iron doors are down to dust,
But the stumps of hinge remain. The arch
Opens to the element—the stones dented
And stained to green and purple and rust.

Pigeons settle on the top. Stranger,
On this winter afternoon pause at the porch,
For the dark land beyond stretches

To the unapproachable element; bright
As night falls and with the allurement of peace,
Concealing under the bland feature, possession.
Not all the agitations of the world
Articulate the ultimate question as do those waters
Confining the memorable and the forgotten;
Relics, records, furtive occasions—Caesar's politics
And he who was drunk last night:
Rings, diamants, snuff boxes, warships,
Also the less worthy garments of worthy men.
Prefer then this handled stone, now ruined

While the sea mists wind about the arch.
The afternoon dwindles, night concludes,
The stone is damp unyielding to the touch,
But crumbling in the strain and stress
Of the years: the years winding about the arch,
Settling in the holes and crevices, moulding
The dressed stone. Once one man bent to it,
Another dropped the measuring line, a third
And fourth positioned to make wall and arch
Theirs. Pause stranger at this small town's edge—
The European sun knew those streets
O Jesu parvule; Christus Victus, Christus Victor,
The bells singing from their towers, the waters
Whispering to the waters, the air tolling
To the air—the faith, the faith, the faith.

All this was long ago. The lights
Are out, the town is sunk in sleep.
The boats are rocking at the pier,
The vague winds beat about the streets—
Choir and altar and chancel are gone.
Under the touch the guardian stone remains
Holding memory, reproving desire, securing hope
In the stop of water, in the lull of night
Before dawn kindles a new day.

LAOTIAN PEASANT SHOT
seen on television war report documentary

He ran in the living air,
exultation in his heels.

A gust of wind will erect
a twisting tower of dried leaves
that will collapse when
the breath is withdrawn.

He turned momentarily,
his eyes looking into his fear,
seeking himself.

When he fell the dust
hung in the air
like an empty container
of him.

UNDER THE MOON

The flowers that fringed the waves
waylaid, sucked his white body
in a wild wash, cut by sharp rocks.
This was the death of a swimmer,
a boy, in November, moonlit.
Lovers, walking on the sands, did not know
his time had run out, theirs being
fulfilled in hushing sound,
turning gently the shells on the beach.
She picked up a fan, a pink shell,
held it transparent before the moon.
'Love, put it in your pocket for me.'
He put her in his pocket. The waves
whisper in her shell ear, 'Love'.

I
Of the five waiters, white, stiff-shirt fronted
With silver trays on the tips of fingers,
At the ready with napkins as white
As their paper faces,
Four were perfect.

The fifth had a shoe-lace untied.
His waxwork tear at his eye
Registered discomfiture,
Conveyed his regret to the single customer
In the corner.

The naphthalene lighting placed the scene;
Edwardian. One
Should not shop at this restaurant
Longer than need be
But pass on to carnage.

II
1914.
He returned in 1917,
His legs bandaged in khaki,
His boots shining new polished.
Marvellous how he had got rid of the trenches.

The only reminder
Was the thin red line at his throat.

III
Now when big-brother Arthur
Stepped
Over our granite doorstep
With his soldier's Balmoral
In his hand

And we had shut the door
On the bright sea

That customarily roared
Outside
And he stood there waiting

For the mother to say
'You're home and no different.'
And the jolly father
To say
'How many Boche this time?'

I put up my finger
To touch the warm flesh
Of the hero who had
Actually killed
A man
And in a good cause.

But there was no difference
In that hand.

LOVE IN AGE

Now that we have had our day, you
having carried, borne children,
been responsible through the wearing years,
in this moment and the next
and still the next as our love
spreads to tomorrow's horizon,
we talk a little before silence.

Let the young make up their love songs,
about which subject they are securely ignorant.
Let them look into eyes that mirror
themselves. Let them groan and ululate
their desire into a microphone. Let them
shout their proclamations over the tannoy
—a whisper is enough for us.

WET SNOW

White tree on black tree,
Ghostly appearance fastened on another,
Called up by harsh spells of this wintry weather
You stand in the night as though to speak to me.

I could almost
Say what you do not fail to say; that's why
I turn away, in terror, not to see
A tree stand there hugged by its own ghost.

NOVEMBER NIGHT, EDINBURGH

The night tinkles like ice in glasses.
Leaves are glued to the pavement with frost.
The brown air fumes at the shop windows,
Tries the doors, and sidles past.

I gulp down winter raw. The heady
Darkness swirls with tenements.
In a brown fuzz of cottonwool
Lamps fade up crags, die into pits.

Frost in my lungs is harsh as leaves
Scraped up on paths.—I look up, there,
A high roof sails, at the mast-head
Fluttering a grey and ragged star.

The world's a bear shrugged in his den.
It's snug and close in the snoring night.
And outside like chrysanthemums
The fog unfolds its bitter scent.

EDINBURGH COURTYARD IN JULY

Hot light is smeared as thick as paint
On these ramshackle tenements. Stones smell
Of dust. Their hoisting into quaint
Crowsteps, corbels, carved with fool and saint,
Holds fathoms of heat, like water in a well.

Cliff-dwellers have poked out from their
High cave-mouths brilliant rags on drying-lines;
They hang still, dazzling in the glare,
And lead the eye up, ledge by ledge, to where
A chimney's tilted helmet winks and shines.

And water from a broken drain
Splashes a glassy hand out in the air
That breaks in an unbraiding rain
And falls still fraying, to become a stain
That spreads by footsteps, ghosting everywhere.

BOATS

The boat need carry no more than a live man
And there's a meaning, a cargo of centuries.
They make a hieroglyph on the sea that can
Cramp circumnavigations in one round gaze.

Hard sailors put out from books and ancient tales.
They have names that chink like gold or clash like ice.
They shred coarse fog or beat suns with their sails,
Pooled in iambics or tossed on hexameters.

Days jagged on skerries, nights signalling with foam
Were golden fleece, white whale, lost Ithaca.
No answering star could call these wanderers home;
Each cape they doubled jutted from history.

Watch this one, ancient Calum. He crabs his boat
Sideways across the tide, every stroke a groan—
Ancient Calum no more, but legends afloat.
No boat ever sailed with a crew of one alone.

89

CELTIC CROSS

The implicated generations made
This symbol of their lives, a stone made light
By what is carved on it.
                        The plaiting masks,
But not with involutions of a shade,
What a stone says and what a stone cross asks.

Something that is not mirrored by nor trapped
In webs of water or bag-nets of cloud;
The tangled mesh of weed
                        lets it go by.
Only men's minds could ever have unmapped
Into abstraction such a territory.

No green bay going yellow over sand
Is written on by winds to tell a tale
Of death-dishevelled gull
                        or heron, stiff
As a cruel clerk with gaunt writs in his hand
—Or even of light, that makes its depths a cliff.

Singing responses order otherwise.
The tangled generations ravelled out
In links of song whose sweet
                        strong choruses
Are these stone involutions to the eyes
Given to the ear in abstract vocables.

The stone remains, and the cross, to let us know
Their unjust, hard demands, as symbols do.
But on them twine and grow
                        beneath the dove
Serpents of wisdom whose cool statements show
Such understanding that it seems like love.

DOUBLE LIFE

This wind from Fife has cruel fingers, scooping
The heat from streets with salty finger-tips
Crusted with frost; and all Midlothian,
Stubborn against what heeled the sides of ships
Off from the Isle of May, stiffens its drooping
Branches to the south. Each man
And woman put their winter masks on, set
In a stony flinch, and only children can
Light with a scream an autumn fire that says
With the quick crackle of its smoky blaze,
'Summer's to burn and it's October yet.'

My Water of Leith runs through a double city;
My city is threaded by a complex stream.
A matter of regret. If these cold stones
Could be stones only, and this watery gleam
Within the chasms of tenements and the pretty
Boskage of Dean could echo the groans
Of cart-wheeled bridges with only water's voice,
October would be just October. The bones
Of rattling winter would still lie underground,
Summer be less than ghost, I be unbound
From all the choking folderols of choice.

A loss of miracles—or an exchange
Of one sort for another. When the trams
Lower themselves like bugs on a branch down
The elbow of the Mound, they'd point the diagrams
Buckled between the New Town and the range
Of the craggy Old: that's all. A noun
Would so usurp all grammar no doing word
Could rob his money-bags or clap a crown
On his turned head, and all at last would be
Existence without category—free
From demonstration except as hill or bird.

And then no double-going stream would sing
Counties and books in the symbolic air,

91

Trundling my forty years to the Port of Leith.
But now, look around, my history's everywhere
And I'm my own environment. I cling
Like a cold limpet underneath
Each sinking stone and am the changing sea.
I die each dying minute and bequeath
Myself to all Octobers and to this
Damned flinty wind that with a scraping kiss
Howls that I'm winter, coming home to me.

BYRE

The thatched roof rings like heaven where mice
Squeak small hosannahs all night long,
Scratching its golden pavements, skirting
The gutter's crystal river-song.

Wild kittens in the world below
Glare with one flaming eye through cracks,
Spurt in the straw, are tawny brooches
Splayed on the chests of drunken sacks.

The dimness becomes darkness as
Vast presences come mincing in,
Swagbellied Aphrodites, swinging
A silver slaver from each chin.

And all is milky, secret, female.
Angels are hushed and plain straws shine.
And kittens miaow in circles, stalking
With tail and hindleg one straight line.

ASSISI

The dwarf with his hands on backwards
Sat, slumped like a half-filled sack
On tiny twisted legs from which
Sawdust might run,

Outside the three tiers of churches built
In honour of St Francis, brother
Of the poor, talker with birds, over whom
He had the advantage
Of not being dead yet.

His look owed its slyness
To the fact
That he had no neck.

A priest explained
How clever it was of Giotto
To make his frescoes tell stories
That would reveal to the illiterate the goodness
Of God and the suffering
Of His Son. I understood
The explanation and
The cleverness.

A rush of tourists, clucking contentedly,
Fluttered after him as he scattered
The grain of the Word.
It was they who had passed
The ruined temple outside, whose eyes
Wept pus, whose back was higher
Than his head, whose lopsided mouth
Said *Grazie* in a voice as sweet
As a child's when she speaks to her mother
Or a bird's when it spoke
To St Francis.

VISITING HOUR

The hospital smell
combs my nostrils
as they go bobbing along
green and yellow corridors.

What seems a corpse
is trundled into a lift and vanishes
heavenward.

I will not feel, I will not
feel, until
I have to.

Nurses walk lightly, swiftly,
here and up and down and there,
their slender waists miraculously
carrying their burden
of so much pain, so
many deaths, their eyes
still clear after
so many farewells.

Ward 7. She lies
in a white cave of forgetfulness.
A withered hand
trembles on its stalk. Eyes move
behind eyelids too heavy
to raise. Into an arm wasted
of colour a glass fang is fixed,
not guzzling but giving.
And between her and me
distance shrinks till there is none left
but the distance of pain that neither she nor I
can cross.

She smiles a little at this
black figure in her white cave
who clumsily rises
in the round swimming waves of a bell
and dizzily goes off, growing fainter,
not smaller, leaving behind only
books that will not be read
and fruitless fruits.

COMPOSERS OF MUSIC

Musicians, calling in your circles and phases,
helpless in their ruminant fire,
unable to speak anything
but the laws of miracles,
how can you fail to shed
your tremulous humanity? How can you carry
your spongebag heart, your ticktocking brain
along those orbits where you go
without skidding—without dying
into the clusters of notes you explode
in the earth's dark mind?

—I regard you with joy and with envy
from my thicket of words.

SLEEPING COMPARTMENT

I don't like this, being carried sideways
through the night. I feel wrong and helpless—like
a timber broadside in a fast stream.

Such a way of moving may suit
that odd snake the sidewinder
in Arizona: but not me in Perthshire.

I feel at right angles to everything,
a crossgrain in existence.—It scrapes
the top of my head, and my footsoles.

To forget outside is no help either—
then I become a blockage
in the long gut of the train.

I try to think I'm a through-the-looking-glass
mountaineer bivouacked
on a ledge five feet high.

It's no good, I go sidelong.
I rock sideways . . . I draw in my feet
to let Aviemore pass.

DAIN DO EIMHIR LIV

Bu tu camhanaich air a' Chuilthionn
's latha suilbhir air a' Chlàraich
grian air a h-uilinn anns an òr-shruth
agus ròs geal bristeadh fàire.

Lainnir sheòl air linne ghrianaich,
gorm a' chuain is iarmailt àr-bhuidh,
an òg-mhaduinn 'na do chùailean
's 'na do ghruaidhean soilleir àlainn.

Mo leug camhanaich is oidhche
t' aodann 's do choibhneas gràdhach,
ged tha bior glas an dòlais
troimh chliabh m' òg-mhaidne sàthte.

YE WERE THE DAWN
from the Gaelic of Sorley Maclean
(Scots version by Douglas Young)

Ye were the dawn on the hills o the Cuillin,
the bousum day on the Clarach arisan,
the sun on his elbucks i the gowden flume,
the whyte rose-fleur that braks the horizon.

Gesserant sails on a skinklan frith,
gowd-yalla lyft and blue o the sea . . .
the fresh mornin in your heid o hair
and your clear face wi its bonnie blee.

Gowdie, my gowdie o dawn and the derk
your loesome gentrice, your brou sae rare . . .
albeid wi the dullyart stang o dule
the breist o youth's been thirlit sair.

DAIN DO EIMHIR XVII

Lìonmhoireachd anns na speuran,
òr-chriathar muillionan de reultan,
fuar, fad as, lòghmhor, àlainn,
tosdach, neo–fhaireachdail, neo–fhàilteach.

Lànachd an eòlais m' an cùrsa,
failmhe an aineolais gun iùl–chairt,
cruinne–cé ag gluasad sàmhach,
aigne leis fhéin anns an àruinn.

Cha n–iadsan a ghluais mo smaointean,
cha n–e mìorbhail an iomchair aognuidh,
cha n–eil a' mhìorbhail ach an gaol duinn,
soillse cruinne an lasadh t'aodainn.

TUMULTUOUS PLENTY IN THE HEAVENS
from the Gaelic of Sorley Maclean
(English version by Iain Crichton Smith)

Tumultuous plenty in the heavens,
gold-sieve of a million stars,
cold, distant, blazing, splendid,
silent and callous in their course.

Fullness of knowledge in their going,
an empty, chartless, ignorant plain.
A universe in soundless motion.
A brooding intellect alone.

It was not they who woke my thinking.
It was not the miracle of their grave
fearful procession, but your face,
a naked universe of love.

CALBHARAIGH

Cha n-eil mo shùil air Calbharaigh
no air Bethlehem an àigh
ach air cùil ghrod an Glaschu
far bheil an lobhadh fàis
agus air seòmar an Dun-éideann,
seòmar bochdainn 's cràidh
far am bheil an naoidhean creuchdach
ri aonagraich gu bhàs.

MY EEN ARE NAE ON CALVARY
from the Gaelic of Sorley Maclean
(Scots version by Douglas Young)

My een are nae on Calvary
or the Bethlehem they praise,
but on shitten back-lands in Glesca toun
whaur growan life decays,
and a stairheid room in an Embro land,
a chalmer o puirtith and skaith,
whaur monie a shilpet bairnikie
gaes smoorit doun til daith.

BAN-GHAIDHEAL

Am faca Tu i, Iùdhaich mhóir,
ri an abrar Aon Mhac Dhe?
Am fac' thu a coltas air Do thriall
ri strì an fhìon-lios chéin?

An cuallach mheasan air a druim,
fallus searbh air mala is gruaidh;
's a' mhìos chreadha trom air cùl
a cinn chrùibte, bhochd, thruaigh.

Chan fhaca Tu i, Mhic an t-saoir,
ri an abrar Rìgh na Glòir,

am measg nan cladach carrach, siar,
fo fhallus cliabh a lòin.

An t-earrach so agus so chaidh
's gach fichead earrach bho an tùs
tharruing ise an fheamainn fhuar
chum biadh a cloinn is duais an tùir.

Is gach fichead foghar tha air triall
chaill i samhradh buidh nam blàth;
is threabh an dubh chosnadh an clais
tarsuinn mìnead ghil a clàir.

Agus labhair T'eaglais chaomh
mu staid chaillte a h-anama thruaigh;
agus leag an cosnadh dian
a corp gu sàmhchair dhuibh an uaigh.

Is thriall a tìm mar shnighe dubh
a' drùdhadh tughaidh fàrdaich bochd;
mheal ise an dubh chosnadh cruaidh;
is glas a cadal suain an nochd.

HIELANT WOMAN
from the Gaelic of Sorley Maclean
(Scots version by Douglas Young)

Hae ye seen her, ye unco Jew,
ye that they caa Ae Son o God?
Thon trauchlit woman i the far vine-yaird,
saw ye the likes o her on your road?

A creelfu o corn upo her spaul,
swyte on her brou, saut swyte on her cheek,
a yirthen pat on the tap o her heid,
her laigh-bouit heid, dwaiblie and sick.

Ye haena seen her, ye son o the vricht,
wi 'King o Glory' fowk roose ye weel,

99

on the staney westland machars thonder
swytan under her wechtit creel.

This spring o the year is by and gane
and twenty springs afore it spent,
sin she's hikeit creels o cauld wrack
for her bairns' meat and the laird's rent.

Twenty hairsts hae dwineit awa,
she's tint her simmer's gowden grace,
while the sair trauchle o the black wark
pleud its rigg on her clear face.

Her puir saul is eternallie tint,
as threeps aye your kindly Kirk;
and endless wark has brocht her corp
to the graff's peace, lown and derk.

Her time gaed by like black sleek
through an auld thaikit hous-rig seepan;
she bruikit aye sair black wark,
and gray the nicht is her lang sleepin.

AN TROM-LAIGHE

Oidhche de'n dà bhliadhna
'N uair shaoil mi gun do chreuchdadh
Mo luaidh le giamh cho miosa
'S a bh'air mnaoi bho linn Eubha,
Bha sinn comhla am bruadar
Ri taobh a' bhalla chloiche
Tha eadar cluich ghart ghillean
Is nighean mo cheud sgoile,
Bha i eadar mo lamhan
'S mo bheul a' dol g'a bilibh
'N uair straon an ceann oillteil
Bho chùl a' bhalla 'n clisgeadh,
Is rinn na cràgan ciara
Fada bréine mo sgornan

A ghlacadh an greim obann
'S lean briathran an eu-dòchais:
'Tha thu ghloic air dheireadh.'

THE WIDDREME
from the Gaelic of Sorley Maclean
(Scots version by Sydney Goodsir Smith)

Ae nicht o thae twa year
Whan I thocht ma luve
Was strak wi a skaith as dure
As wumman's had sen Eve,
We were thegither in a dwaum
By the stane dyke that staunds
Atween the loons' and lassies' yairds
O ma first schuil.
                    Ma airms
Were round her and ma lips
Seekan her mou
Whan the laithlie gorgon's heid stuid up
On a sudden frae hint the waa,
And the lang mirk ugsome fingers graipt
Ma craig wi a sudden grup—
And then the words o weirdless dule:
'Owre blate, ye fuil!'

HALLAIG
'Tha tìm, am fiadh, an coille Hallaig'

Tha bùird is tàirnean air an uinneig
troimh 'm faca mi an Aird an Iar
's tha mo ghaol aig Allt Hallaig
'na craoibh bheithe, 's bha i riamh

eadar an t-Inbhir 's Poll a' Bhainne,
thall 's a bhos mu Bhaile-Chùirn:
tha i 'na beithe, 'na calltuinn,
'na caorunn dhìreach sheang ùir.

101

Ann an Screapadal mo chinnidh,
far robh Tarmad 's Eachunn Mór,
tha 'n nigheanan 's am mic 'nan coille
ag gabhail suas ri taobh an loin.
Uaibhreach a nochd na coilich ghiuthais
ag gairm air mullach Cnoc an Rà,
dìreach an druim ris a' ghealaich—
chan iadsan coille mo ghràidh.

Fuirichidh mi ris a' bheithe
gus an tig i mach an Càrn,
gus am bi am bearradh uile
o Bheinn na Lice f' a sgàil.

Mura tig 's ann theàrnas mi a Hallaig
a dh' ionnsaigh sàbaid nam marbh,
far a bheil an sluagh a' tathaich,
gach aon ghinealach a dh' fhalbh.

Tha iad fhathast ann a Hallaig,
Clann Ghill-Eain 's Clann MhicLeoid,
na bh' ann ri linn Mhic Ghille-Chaluim:
Chunnacas na mairbh beò.

Na fir 'nan laighe air an lianaig
aig ceann gach taighe a bh' ann,
na nigheanan 'nan coille bheithe,
dìreach an druim, crom an ceann.

Eadar an Leac is na Feàrnaibh
tha 'na rathad mór fo chóinnich chiùin,
's na nigheanan 'nam badan sàmhach
a' dol a Chlachan mar o thùs.

Agus a' tilleadh as a' Chlachan,
á Suidhisnis 's á tir nam beò;
a chuile té òg uallach
gun bhristeadh cridhe an sgeòil.

O Allt na Feàrnaibh gus an fhaoilinn
tha soilleir an dìomhaireachd nam beann
chan eil ach coimhthional nan nighean
ag cumail na coiseachd gun cheann.

A' tilleadh a Hallaig anns an fheasgar,
anns a' chamhanaich bhalbh bheò,
a' lìonadh nan leathadan casa,
an gàireachdaich 'nam chluais 'na ceò,

's am bòidhche 'na sgleò air mo chridhe
mun tig an ciaradh air na caoil,
's nuair theàrnas grian air cùl Dhun Cana
thig peileir dian á gunna Ghaoil;

's buailear am fiadh a tha 'na thuaineal
a' snòtach nan làraichean feòir;
thig reothadh air a shùil 'sa choille:
chan fhaighear lorg air fhuil ri m' bheo.

HALLAIG
'Time, the deer, is in the wood of Hallaig'

The window is nailed and boarded
Through which I saw the West
And my love is at the Burn of Hallaig
A birch tree, and she has always been

Between Inver and Milk Hollow,
Here and there about Baile-chuirn:
She is a birch, a hazel,
A straight slender young rowan.

In Screapadal of my people,
Where Norman and Big Hector were,
Their daughters and their sons are a wood
Going up beside the stream.

Proud tonight the pine cocks
Crowing on the top of Cnoc an Rà
Straight their backs in the moonlight—
They are not the wood I love.

I will wait for the birch wood
Until it comes up by the Cairn,
Until the whole ridge from Beinn na Lice
Will be under its shade.

If it does not, I will go down to Hallaig,
To the sabbath of the dead,
Where the people are frequenting,
Every single generation gone.

They are still in Hallaig,
MacLeans and MacLeods,
All who were there in the time of Mac Gille Chaluim:
The dead have been seen alive.

The men lying on the green
At the end of every house that was,
The girls a wood of birches,
Straight their backs, bent their heads.

Between the Leac and Fearns
The road is under mild moss
And the girls in silent bands
Go to Clachan as in the beginning.

And return from Clachan,
From Suisnish and the land of the living;
Each one young and light-stepping,
Without the heartbreak of the tale

From the Burn of Fearns to the raised beach
That is clear in the mystery of the hills,
There is only the congregation of the girls
Keeping up the endless walk.

Coming back to Hallaig in the evening,
In the dumb living twilight,
Filling the steep slopes,
Their laughter in my ears a mist,

And their beauty a film on my heart
Before the dimness comes on the kyles,
And when the sun goes down behind Dun Cana
A vehement bullet will come from the gun of love;

And will strike the deer that goes dizzily,
Sniffing at the grass-grown ruined homes;
His eye will freeze in the wood;
His blood will not be traced while I live.

J.F. HENDRY

INVERBEG

Sliced with shade and scarred with snow
A mountain breaks like Mosaic rock
And through the lilt of mist there flow
Restless rivers of pebble, pocked
And speckled, where moss and the centuries grow.

Tree, married to cloud as stem is to feather,
Branches and straddles the convex of sky.
Death is aflame in the bracken where heather
Rears semaphore smoke into high
Blue messenger fire through soundless weather.

Below, like bees, the ivies swarm,
Cast in leaping veins, their trunk, a crippled
Animal of thighs pounced from loch-water, storms
The slated shores of the past into ripples
Interpreting man's fretted cuneiform.

THE SHIP

Here is a ship you made
Out of my breasts and sides
As I lay dead in the yards
Under the hammers.

Here is the hull you built
Out of a heart of salt,
Sky-rent, the prey of birds
Strung on the longshore.

Here is her rigging bound
Nerve, sinew, ice and wind
Blowing though the night
The starred dew of beads.

Here her ribs of silver
Once steerless in a culvert
Climb the laddered centuries
To hide a cloud in a frame.

THE CONSTANT NORTH
(For Dee)

Encompass me, my lover,
With your eyes' wide calm.
Though noonday shadows are assembling doom,
The sun remains when I remember them;
And death, if it should come,
Must fall like quiet snow from such clear skies.

Minutes we snatched from the unkind winds
Are grown into daffodils by the sea's
Edge, mocking its green miseries;
Yet I seek you hourly still, over
A new Atlantis loneliness, blind
As a restless needle held by the constant north we always
    have in mind.

106

THE FALLS OF FALLOCH

This white explosion of water plunges down
With the deep-voiced rush of sound that shakes a city.
A fine cold smoke drifts across dripping stone
And wet black walls of rock shut in the scene.

Now thought hangs sheer on a precipice of beauty
Lifting with leaping water out from the rock.
A gasp of time, flung clear in a weight of falling,
Bursts like a bud above the deep pool's black
Parted and curled back under by the shock
Where light's bright spark dives to the dark's controlling.

But the brilliance is not extinguished. The heart leaps up,
The heart of the fall leaps up, an eternal explosion,
Force without spending, form without fetter of shape.
And at the pool's edge wavelets scarcely lap
Where drifted spume clings with a soft adhesion.

REMOTE COUNTRY

The way goes snaking upward through the heat.
Out of the carving river's narrow space
Shaken with noise of water, black and white,
You climb at last into a scooped-out place
Where nothing moves but wind treading grass.

All cover's past. Below, the waterfalls
Dig out of sight, like memory. You stare up,
Strange in this trap ringed all about by hills,
To find the one way out, confined and steep,
Watched by whatever eyes look from the top.

When you have crossed the open, reached the height,
It is a brown plateau, cratered and bare,
Low, lumpy hills and black, eroded peat

Stretching as far as light can throw its glare,
No living thing in sight in sky or moor.

Mind finds its way to meet with solitude.
Bear this in mind: the image will not age
Of desert, light and always moving cloud.
It is a vision to exhaust all rage.
Calculate nothing. Leave an empty page.

NORTH OF BERWICK

Slowly the sea is parted from the sky:
The light surprises, crinkling on the water.
The white sun hardens; cliffs solidify.
A long coast of red rock where three swans fly
Engraves itself in calm, deceptive weather.

Three swans fly north, a diesel thumping south
Draws out of sight along the rusting railway,
All windows clouded with a communal breath.
Fields flash in the sunlight, far beneath
The sea turns in its scales, well in a seal's way.

No boat invades that shining emptiness.
Because the waves are distant, the sky windless,
That pale line round the shore looks motionless.
Hearing such border warfare lost in space
You say the breathing of the sea is endless.

What is the one thing constant? Can you say?
The loneliness that we are born to merges
Perhaps with such a place on such a day.
No stones cry out because we cannot stay.
Through all our absences the long tide surges.

THE GALLOWAY SHORE

Sand white as frost: the moon stayed hard and high.
Far off, the lights around the Irish coast
Leapt up like salmon. An Iscariot sea
Chinked on the rocks. Within a shadow cast
By broken cliffs, a place of slippery stones,
I faced the speaking lights, small human signs
Of hidden rocks and granite patiences.
Among the sounds of night a slithering wind,
Darkness on dark, in fitful cadences
Phrased the fresh world. There is no older sound.

Never was stillness here, where I began
To watch alone, to be an emptiness,
To let the strongly running world come in
As seldom can be done: this was to pass
Into no trance but a most brilliant waking,
Active as light upon the deep tide snaking
Before my sight, so lately lost in crowds.
The force that moves all things and lives me out
Made me its filament; all that divides
Time into stints could be no longer thought.

To be had no past tense: all sense was new.
There was destruction of irrelevance.
A listener to the world, I heard it flow
So huge, so slow, it seemed like permanence
Experienced for an eye-blink. Darting knives
Made slits of light. My years, those forty thieves
Crowded together in one brimming jar,
Left me no wish to grieve for. All this hoard
Was poured out in an instant to the air,
While I was bankrupt even of a word.

Was it some trick to steal the peace of the dead?
It was not peace but power, surely the source
Of every light lit in a transient head
From Genesis to Einstein. In this place
(Austere, coherent, callous) all deeds done,

Bastilles of knowledge, crumpled. The moon's lane,
Quickened with silver, ran; all near was dark,
The land behind most dark. Spread round the sea,
Pinpricks of light timed out a few men's work,
Wakeful in cells impenetrable by me.

Our time seeks for an idol. There is none.
The image that you want is not a city,
Nothing so pitiable; the sea pours in
And shears your dwellings down, ignores your duty
To house a purpose, bears you to extreme.
The lights were warning lights by which I came
As polar travellers come to what is real
In all their banished days. The sight was calm.
There is not any will, or wall, or cell
Would keep this calmness out. Give it no name.

Growing, the poem's dumb, planted in change
Immeasurable and ineluctable.
It flowers in light. We reach outside our range
Into the sureness, indestructible,
That sings us out of time. Whose is our voice?
It is the voice of stones that waste, of seas
That cannot rest, of air transfixed by light:
That is to say a human voice, that tries,
Always in solitude, aided by night,
To be identified with all of these.

The sun's white shadow darkened all the sea
With cool and bearable light. I knew this dark;
It was the earth between me and the day
And this my turning place, a boundary mark.
The brittle sea fractured along the coast.
The Irish lights jigged on, fixed points that placed
My world on stone foundations. They put space
A little farther off where men marooned
In granite kept their watch. The moon was glass.
I leaned against a rock, out of the wind.

MIXED WEATHER

The holly leaves are glinting in the sun.
Thumped by the wind half senseless we come in,
Into our wits and out of part of our senses,
To watch how the light dances
And lie to ourselves that the long winter's done.

The naked trees roll wildly. Hedges lean
Ready to take off smartly from the scene.
Shadows, dead leaves and flurries of snow are flying.
All fixity's for denying
And wind blurts at the door like a trombone.

Forty-foot cherry trees lie on the ground
Roots raised like horns, no more to be earthbound.
The sky is blue and white and dark and glowing.
A rock in the tide's flowing,
The hill is hit by wave upon wave of sound.

At last the sun goes down, an orange blaze,
The night takes over with a darker noise.
My collie dog who wags his tail in sleeping
Feels he is in safe keeping
Lacking the fearful forethought we call wise.

Lock the door, trusting that it won't blow in.
Hear how the world's alive. The haring moon
Breaks cover and goes tearing into space,
Space that is like packed ice
With all the furies yelling out of tune.

SABBATH I THE MEARNS

The geans are fleuran whyte i the green Howe o the Mearns;
wastlan winds are blawan owre the Mownth's cauld glacks,
whaur the whaups wheep round their nesties among the
    fog and ferns;
and the ferm-touns stand gray and lown, ilk wi its yalla
    stacks.
The kirk is skailan, and the fowk in Sabbath stand o blacks
are doucely haudan hame til their denners wi the bairns,
the young anes daffan and auld neebours haean cracks.

Thon's bien and canty livin for auld-farrant fermer-fowk
wha wark their lives out on the land, the bonnie Laigh o
    Mearns.
They pleu and harra, saw and reap, clatt neeps and tattie-
    howk,
and dinna muckle fash theirsels wi ither fowk's concerns.
There's whiles a chyld that's unco wild, but sune the
    wildest learns
gin ye're nae a mensefu fermer-chiel ye's be naething but
    a gowk,
and the auld weys are siccar, auld and siccar like the sterns.

They werena aye like thon, this auld Albannach race,
whas stanes stand heich upo' the Mownth whaur the wild
    whaup caas.
Focht for libertie wi Wallace, luikit tyrants i the face,
stuid a siege wi leal Ogilvie for Scotland's king and laws,*
i the Whigs' Vaut o Dunnottar testified for Freedom's
    cause.
Is there onie Hope to equal the Memories o this place?
The last Yerl Marischal's deid, faan doun his castle waas.

---

* Sir George Ogilvie of Barras held Dunnottar Castle, with Charles II's
regalia inside, against the Cromwellian General Monk.

LUVE

Gie aa, and aa comes back
　wi mair nor aa.
Hain ocht, and ye'll hae nocht,
　aa flees awa.

hain ocht—keep anything　　hae nocht—have nothing

FOR A WIFE IN JIZZEN

Lassie, can ye say
　whaur ye ha been,
whaur ye ha come frae,
　whatna ferlies seen?

Eftir the bluid and swyte,
　the warsslin o yestreen,
ye ligg forfochten, whyte,
　prouder nor onie queen.

Albeid ye hardly see me
　I read it i your een,
sae saft blue and dreamy,
　mindan whaur ye've been.

Anerly wives ken
　the ruits o joy and tene,
　　the march o daith and birth,
　　　the tryst o luve and strife
i the howedumbdeidsunsheen,
　　fire, air, water, yirth
　　　mellan to mak new life,
　　lauchan and greetan, feiman and serene.

Dern frae aa men
　the ferlies ye ha seen.

ferlies—marvels　　warsslin—wrestling, struggle　　ligg—lie　　forfochten—
exhausted by struggle　　tene—sorrow　　march—boundary　　howe-
dumbdeidsunsheen—sunshine at dead of night　　mellan—encountering
lauchan—laughing　　greetan—crying　　feiman—in violent heat and
commotion　　dern—hidden, secret

113

FOR THE OLD HIGHLANDS

That old lonely lovely way of living
in Highland places,—twenty years a-growing,
twenty years flowering, twenty years declining,—
father to son, mother to daughter giving
ripe tradition; peaceful bounty flowing;
one harmony all tones of life combining,—
old wise ways, passed like the dust blowing.

That harmony of folk and land is shattered,—
the yearly rhythm of things, the social graces,
peat-fire and music, candle-light and kindness.
Now they are gone it seems they never mattered,
much, to the world, those proud and violent races,
clansmen, and chiefs whose passioned greed and blindness
made desolate these lovely lonely places.

THE SHEPHERD'S DOCHTER

Lay her and lea her here i the gantan grund,
    the blythest, bonniest lass o the countryside,
    crined in a timber sark, hapt wi the pride
o hothous flouers, the dearest that could be fund.

Her faither and brithers stand, as suddentlie stunned
    wi the wecht o dule; douce neebours side by side
    wreist and fidge, sclent-luikan, sweirt tae bide
while the Minister's duin and his threep gane wi the wind.

The murners skail, thankfu tae lea thon place
    whar the blythest, bonniest lass liggs in the mouls,
    Lent lilies lowp and cypresses stand stieve,
    Time tae gae back tae the darg, machines and tools
        and beasts and seeds, the things men uis tae live,
and lea the puir lass there in her state o Grace.

gantan—gaping   wreist—shift about uneasily   threep—talk   skail—
disperse   mouls—clay

ON A NORTH BRITISH DEVOLUTIONARY

They libbit William Wallace,
   he gart them bleed.
They dinna libb MacFoozle,
   they dinna need.

libbit—castrated

LAST LAUCH

The Minister said it wald dee,
   the cypress buss I plantit.
But the buss grew til a tree,
   naething dauntit.

It's growan stark and heich,
   derk and straucht and sinister,
kirkyairdie-like and dreich.
   But whaur's the Minister?

buss—bush

RUTHVEN TODD

ABOUT SCOTLAND, & C.

I was my own ghost that walked among the hills,
Strolled easily among the ruined stones of history;
The student of geography, concerned with fells
And screes rather than with the subtle mystery
Of action's causes—the quickly overbalanced rock
Upon the passing victim, the stab in the back.

Why did this burn run that way to the sea,
Digging a cutting through stone, moss and peat,
And so become ingredient of whisky?
Why was this glen the cause of a defeat,
The silver bullet in the young man's lung,
The devil's puppet and hero of a song?

That queen herself was lorded by the weather,
And Knox drew sustenance from poverty,
The sharp east wind, the sickle in the heather.
The reiver was cornered in the sudden sortie
Of armoured men lying hidden in the bracken,
And a royal line was by sea-storm broken.

This way the landscape formed the people,
Controlled their deeds with cairn and gully;
And no pretender or well-favoured noble
Had power like dammed loch or empty valley.
Their history's origins lie in rock and haze
And the hero seems shorter than his winter days.

This my ghost saw from the deserted keep
And the left paper-mill forgotten in the slums,
This he saw south among the soft-fleshed sheep
And north-west where the Atlantic drums.
Then, since he'd made no claim to be apostle,
He left, his trophy a neglected fossil.

PERSONAL HISTORY
for my son

O my heart is the unlucky heir of the ages
And my body is unwillingly the secret agent
Of my ancestors; those content with their wages
From history: the Cumberland Quaker whose gentle
Face was framed with lank hair to hide the ears
Cropped as a punishment for his steadfast faith,
The Spanish lady who had seen the pitch lake's broth
In the West Indian island and the Fife farmers
To whom the felted barley meant a winter's want.

My face presents my history, and its sallow skin
Is parchment for the Edinburgh lawyer's deed:
To have and hold in trust, as feoffee therein
Until such date as the owner shall have need
Thereof. My brown eyes are jewels I cannot pawn,

And my long lip once curled beside an Irish bog,
My son's whorled ear was once my father's, then mine;
I am the map of a campaign, each ancestor has his flag
Marking an advance or a retreat. I am their seed.

As I write I look at the five fingers of my hand,
Each with its core of nacre bone, and rippled nails;
Turn to the palm and the traced unequal lines that end
In death—only at the tips my ancestry fails—
The dotted swirls are original and are my own:
Look at this fringed polyp which I daily use
And ask its history, ask to what grave abuse
It has been put: perhaps it curled about the stone
Of Cain. At least it has known much of evil,

And perhaps as much of good, been tender
When tenderness was needed, and been firm
On occasion, and in its past been free of gender,
Been the hand of a mother holding the warm
Impress of the child against her throbbing breast,
Been cool to the head inflamed in fever,
Sweet and direct in contact with a lover.
O in its cupped and fluted shell lies all the past;
My fingers close about the crash of history's storm.

In the tent of night I hear the voice of Calvin
Expending his hatred of the world in icy words;
Man less than a red ant beneath the towering mountain,
And God a troll more fearful than the feudal lords;
The Huguenots in me, flying Saint Bartholomew's Day,
Are in agreement with all this, and their resentful hate
Flames brighter than the candles on an altar, the grey
Afternoon is lit by catherine wheels of terror, the street
Drinks blood and pity in death before their swords

The cantilever of my bones acknowledges the architect,
My father, to whom always the world was a mystery
Concealed in the humped base of a bottle, one solid fact
To set against the curled pages and the tears of history.

117

I am a Border keep, a croft and a solicitor's office,
A country rectory, a farm and a drawing-board:
In me, as in so many, the past has stored its miser's hoard,
Won who knows where nor with what loaded dice.
When my blood pulses it is their blood I feel hurry.

These forged me, the latest link in a fertile chain
With ends that run so far that my short sight
Cannot follow them, nor can my weak memory claim
Acquaintance with the earliest shackle. In my height
And breadth I hold my history, and then my son
Holds my history in his small body and the history of
    another,
Who for me has no contact but that of flesh, his mother.
What I make now I make, indeed, from the unknown,
A blind man spinning furiously in the web of night.

IT WAS EASIER

Now over the map that took ten million years
Of rain and sun to crust like boiler-slag,
The lines of fighting men progress like caterpillars,
Impersonally looping between the leaf and twig.

One half of the map is shaded as if by night
Or an eclipse. It is difficult from far away
To understand that a man's booted feet
May grow blistered marching there, or a boy

Die from a bullet. It is difficult to plant
That map with olives, oranges or grapes,
Or to see men alive at any given point,
To see dust-powdered faces or cracked lips.

It is easier to avoid all thought of it
And shelter in the elegant bower of legend,
To dine in dreams with kings, to float
Down the imaginary river, crowds on each hand

Cheering each mention of my favoured name.
It is easier to collect anecdotes, the tall tales
That travellers, some centuries ago, brought home,
Or wisecracks and the drolleries of fools;

It is easier to sail paper-boats on lily-ponds,
To plunge like a gannet in the sheltered sea,
To go walking or to chatter with my friends
Or to discuss the rare edition over tea,

Than to travel in the mind to that place
Where the map becomes reality, where cracks
Are gullies, a bullet more than half-an-inch
Of small newsprint and the shaped grey rocks

Are no longer the property of wandering painters,
A pleasant watercolour for an academic wall,
But cover for the stoat-eyed snipers
Whose aim is fast and seldom known to fail.

It is easier . . . but no, the map has grown
And now blocks out the legends, the sweet dreams
And the chatter. The map has come alive. I hear the moan
Of the black planes and see their pendant bombs.

I can no longer hide in fancy: they'll hunt me out.
That map has mountains and these men have blood:
'Time has an answer!' cries my familiar ghost,
Stirred by explosives from his feather bed.

Time may have answers but the map is here.
Now is the future that I never wished to see.
I was quite happy dreaming and had no fear:
But now, from the map, a gun is aimed at me.

BROKEN ARROWHEADS AT CHILMARK, MARTHA'S VINEYARD

Glint of white quartz on the pale cream sand,
Or sparkle of worked stone, red, black or green;
The eye, unwillingly trapped, impels the hand
To weigh these fragments of what once had been.

Here then there sat the knapper of the flint,
With fire and careful tap he shaped the head;
From this dark pit he drew stone without stint,
Stones for his working. But he has been dead

A long time. The nickel case of the twenty-two
Corrodes in the salt air. The Indian on relief,
Or plumbing, is hardly the same Indian who
Discarded his failures without petulance or grief.

Perhaps the working of quartz was waste of time;
But such waste and inefficiency could contrive
Lastingness—the paper shell-case moulders into grime.
These sharp and many coloured chips survive

While rain and storms erode and centuries elide.
Efficiency seems trivial and our artefacts must pass
As impermanent symbols that cannot lie beside
The arrowhead in the clump of blue-eyed grass.

G.S. FRASER

TO HUGH MACDIARMID

Since mine was never the heroic gesture,
    Trained to slick city from my childhood's days,
Only a rambling garden's artful leisure
    Giving my mind its privacy and ease.

Since Poverty for me has never sharpened
    Her single tooth, and since Adversity

So far has failed to jab me with her hair-pin,
    I marvel who my Scottish Muse can be.

I am Convention's child, the cub reporter,
    The sleek, the smooth, conservatively poised:
Abandoned long ago by Beauty's daughter;
    Tamed like a bronco, and commercialized!

Perhaps I have a heart that feels. . . . I wonder!
    At least I can salute your courage high,
Your thought that burns language to a cinder,
    Your anger, and your angry poet's joy.

O warrior, with the world and wind against you,
    Old sea-bird, in your bleak and rocky coign,
Only my fears can follow where you fly to . . .
    Beneath these rocks, how many souls lie slain!

Your journey has not been the private journey
    Through a mad loveliness, of Hölderlin.
Against the windmills, sir, you chose to tourney.
    And yet, by marvellous chance, you hold your own.

O true bright sword! Perhaps, like Mithridates,
    Before the night has fallen, you may say:
'Now I am satisfied: at least my hate is:
    Now let me die: I saw the English flee.'

Facing boys' faces, whom your world of thunder
    Is massing clouds for, whom the violet forks
Seek out from heaven . . . simulating candour
    I face both ways! A secret question carks.

Because my love was never for the common
    But only for the rare, the singular air,
Or the undifferenced and naked human,
    Your Keltic mythos shudders me with fear.

What a race has is always crude and common,
    And not the human or the personal:
I would take sword up only for the human,
    Not to revive the broken ghosts of Gael.

LEAN STREET

Here, where the baby paddles in the gutter,
    Here, in the slaty greyness and the gas,
Here, where the women wear dark shawls and mutter
    A hasty word as other women pass.

Telling the secret, telling, clucking and tutting,
    Sighing, or saying that it served her right,
The bitch!—the words and weather both are cutting
    In Causewayend, on this November night.

At pavement's end and in the slaty weather
    I stare with glazing eyes at meagre stone,
Rain and the gas are sputtering together
    A dreary tune! O leave my heart alone,

O leave my heart alone, I tell my sorrows,
    For I will soothe you in a softer bed
And I will numb your grief with fat tomorrows
    Who break your milk teeth on this stony bread!

They do not hear. Thought stings me like an adder,
    A doorway's sagging plumb-line squints at me,
The fat sky gurgles like a swollen bladder
    With the foul rain that rains on poverty.

HOMETOWN ELEGY
(for Aberdeen in Spring)

Glitter of mica at the windy corners,
Tar in the nostrils, under blue lamps budding
Like bubbles of glass and blue buds of a tree,
Night-shining shopfronts, or the sleek sun flooding
The broad abundant dying sprawl of the Dee:
For these and for their like my thoughts are mourners
That yet shall stand, though I come home no more,
Gas works, white ballroom, and the red brick baths
And salmon nets along a mile of shore,
Or beyond the municipal golf-course, the moorland paths

And the country lying quiet and full of farms.
This is the shape of a land that outlasts a strategy
And is not to be taken with rhetoric or arms.
Or my own room, with a dozen books on the bed
(Too late, still musing what I mused, I lie
And read too lovingly what I have read),
Brantôme, Spinoza, Yeats, the bawdy and wise,
Continuing their interminable debate,
With no conclusion, they conclude too late,
When their wisdom has fallen like a grey pall on my eyes.
Syne we maun part, there sall be nane remeid—
Unless my country is my pride, indeed,
Or I can make my town that homely fame
That Byron has, from boys in Carden Place,
Struggling home with books to midday dinner,
For whom he is not the romantic sinner,
The careless writer, the tormented face,
The hectoring bully or the noble fool,
But, just like Gordon or like Keith, a name:
A tall, proud statue at the Grammar School.

HE DEATH OF MY GRANDMOTHER

There's little personal grief in a quiet old death:
Grief for a landscape dying in our heads,
Knowing how London melts us to her style.

What if she got those touches in her talk
(The half-impression of a scene that had
Flowed in her youthful blood and set as bone)
From phrases in some novel by John Buchan?
A memory is other than the words for it:
Persistence was her gift, not literature,
A character no town could penetrate,
Not Glasgow's sprawl, nor London's repetitions—
No more that landscape now: no more the old
Books in the glass case, and the box bed
I half remember as a boy in Glasgow:
Caithness enclosed within a house in Glasgow,

Glasgow enclosed in London: time in time,
The past within the past, parentheses.
In laying her to rest, it is as if
We folded up with her brown age a landscape,
A ribbed and flat and rocky map of duty
That is the northern edge of every island
Where pleasure flowers only in the swollen south:
Mourn character that could persist so long
Where softer personality dies young.

These lights and glimpses lost now: only bones,
Shapes of our heads, only the arguing voice,
In a foreign milieu the improvised fine manners.

Think of those rock-stacks in the stony Orkneys
That, toppling, stand improbably for years,
The sea persisting at them: and at last,
Boys' bricks, they crash on the untidy beach.
So with her piled and uncemented past:
Its tottering tower seemed out of the tide's reach.
Time merely fretted at the base. No more
Of all the colour of her years was hers
Than brown rock's is blue sea's. O travellers,
Who take the stain of Time, as I have done,
Expose your fluctuations to the sun:
Yet, for such stony virtue, spare your tears.

THE TRAVELLER HAS REGRETS

The traveller has regrets
For the receding shore
That with its many nets
Has caught, not to restore,
The white lights in the bay,
The blue lights on the hill,
Though night with many stars
May travel with him still,
But night has nought to say,

Only a colour and shape
Changing like cloth shaking,
A dancer with a cape
Whose dance is heart-breaking,
Night with its many stars
Can warn travellers
There's only time to kill
And nothing much to say:
But the blue lights on the hill,
The white lights in the bay
Told us the meal was laid
And that the bed was made
And that we could not stay.

R. CROMBIE SAUNDERS

THE EMPTY GLEN

Time ticks away the centre of my pride
Emptying its glen of cattle, crops, and song,
Till its deserted headlands are alone
Familiar with the green uncaring tide.

What gave this land to gradual decay?
The rocky field where plovers make their nest
Now undisturbed had once the soil to raise
A happy people, but from day to day

The hamlets failed, the young men sought the towns,
Bewildered age looked from the cottage door
Upon the wreck of all they'd laboured for,
The rotting gate, the bracken on the downs;

And wondered if the future was so black
The children would have stayed but did not dare,
Who might, they hoped, be happy where they are.
And wondered, Are they ever coming back?

LOCH LEVEN

Tell me was a glorie ever seen
As the morn I left ma lass
'Fore licht i the toun o snaw
And saw the daw
O' burnan crammassie
Turn the grey ice
O' Mary's Loch Leven
To sheenan bress—
An kent the glorie and the gleen
Was but the waukenin o her een?

LARGO

Ae boat anerlie nou
Fishes frae this shore,
Ae black drifter lane,
Riggs the cramasie daw—
Aince was a fleet, but nou
Ae boat alane gaes out.

War or peace, the trawlers win
And the youth turns awa
Bricht wi baubles nou
And thirled to factory or store;
Their faithers fished their ain,
Unmaistered; ane remains.

And never the clock rins back,
The free days are owre;
The warld shrinks, we luik
Mair t'oor maisters ilka hour—
Whan yon lane boat I see
Daith and rebellion blinn ma ee.

thirled—attached to

SPLEEN

Steir bogle, squat bogle
Bogle o sweirness and stuperie;
Wersh bogle, wae bogle,
Bogle o drumlie apathie;
Thir twa haud this fule in duress—
Malancolie, Idleness.

In duress vile ye muckle fule,
Cock o your midden o sloth and stour,
Geck o the yill and a restless saul
I dwaum lik a convict, dowf and dour
As the runt o a riven aik
Whaur ghouls can sit or their hurdies ache.

THE GRACE OF GOD AND THE METH-DRINKER

There ye gang, ye daft
And doitit dotterel, ye saft
Crazed outland skalrag saul
In your bits and ends o winnockie duds
Your fyled and fozie-fousome clouts
As fou's a fish, crackt and craftie-drunk
Wi bleerit reid-rimmed
Ee and slaveran crozie mou
Dwaiblan owre the causie like a ship
Storm-toss't i' the Bay of Biscay O
At-sea indeed and hauf-seas-owre
Up-til-the-thrapple's-pap
Or up-til-the-crosstrees-sunk—
    Wha kens? Wha racks?

Hidderie-hetterie stouteran in a dozie dwaum
O' ramsh reid-biddie—Christ!
    The stink
O' jake ahint him, a mephitic
Rouk o miserie, like some unco exotic
Perfume o the Orient no juist sae easilie tholit

By the bleak barbarians o the Wast
But subtil, acrid, jaggan the nebstrous
Wi'n owrehailan ugsome guff, maist delicat,
Like in scent til the streel o a randie gib. . . .
    O-hone-a-ree!

His toothless gums, his lips, bricht cramasie
A scheer-bricht slash o bluid
A schene like the leaman gleid o rubies
Throu the gray-white stibble
O' his blank unrazit chafts, a hangman's
Heid, droolie wi gob, the bricht een
Sichtless, cannie, blythe, and slee—
                                    Unkennan.

Ay,
    Puir gangrel!
                There
—But for the undeemous glorie and grace
O' a mercifu omnipotent majestie God
Superne eterne and sceptred in the firmament
Whartil the praises o the leal rise
Like incense aye about Your throne,
Ayebydan, thochtless, and eternallie hauf-drunk
Wi nectar, Athole-brose, ambrosia—nae jake for You—
                                    God, there!—
But for the 'bunesaid unsocht grace, unprayed for,
Undeserved—
                Gangs,
                    Unregenerate,
                            Me.

winnockie duds—ragged clothes   ramsh reid-biddie—meths and urine
mixed   streel—urine   gib—tom-cat   leaman gleid—blazing flames

ELEGY XIII
(from *Under the Eildon Tree*)

(i)
I got her in the Black Bull
(The Black Bull o Norroway),
Gin I mynd richt, in Leith Street,

Doun the stair at the corner forenent
The Fun Fair and Museum o Monstrosities,
   The Tyke-faced Loun, the Cunyiars Den
      And siclike.
I tine her name the nou, and cognomen for that—
Aiblins it was Deirdre, Ariadne, Calliope,
Gaby, Jacquette, Katerina, Sandra,
   Or sunkots; exotic, I expeck.
A wee bit piece
   O' what our faithers maist unaptlie
   But romanticallie designatit 'Fluff'.
My certie! Nae muckle o fluff
   About the hures o Reekie!
Dour as stane, the like stane
As biggit the unconquerable citie
Whar they pullulate,
               Infestan
The wynds and closes, squares
And public promenads
    —The bonnie craturies!
        —But til our winter's tale.

(ii)
Fou as a puggie, I, the bardic ee
In a fine frenzie rollan,
Drunk as a fish wi sevin tails,
Purpie as Tiberio wi bad rum and beerio,
      (Io! Io! Iacche! Iacche, Io!)
—Sevin nichts and sevin days
     (A modest bout whan aa's dune,
     Maist scriptural, in fack)
Was the Makar on his junketins
     (On this perticular occasioun
     O' the whilk we tell the nou
      Here in the records, for the benefit
      O' future putative historians)
Wi sindrie cronies throu the wastage-land
O' howffs and dancins, stews
And houses o assignatioun
I' the auntient capital.

—Ah, she was a bonnie cou!
Ilka pennie I had she teuk,
Scoffed the halicarnassus lot,
As is the custom, due
And meet and mensefu,
Proper and proprietous,
    Drinkan hersel to catch up wi me
    That had a sevin-day stert on her
        —O' the whilk conditioun
Nae smaa braggandie was made at the time
Here and yont about the metropolis—
    And mysel drinkan me sober again
For reasouns ower obvious
To needcessitate descriptioun,
                    Explanatioun,
                    Or ither.

Nou, ye canna ging lang at yon game
And the hour cam on at length
That the Cup-bearer did refuse
The provision of further refreshment
—Rochlie, I mynd, and in a menner
Wi the whilk I amna uised,
    Unconformable wi my lordlie spreit,
    A menner unseemlie, unbefittan
    The speakin-til or interlocutioun
    O' a Bard and Shennachie,
        Far less a Maister o Arts,
        —The whilk rank and statioun I haud
        In consequence and by vertue
        O' unremittan and pertinacious
        Applicatioun til the bottle
        Ower a period no exceedan
        Fowr year and sax munce or moneths
(The latter bean a *hiatus* or *caesura*
For the purposes o rusticatioun
Or *villeggiatura* 'at my place in the country'):
    Aa the whilk was made sufficient plain
Til the Cup-bearer at the time—
    Losh me, what a collieshangie!

Ye'd hae thocht the man affrontit
  Deeplie, maist mortallie
    And til the hert.
Ay, and I cried him Ganymede,
  Wi the whilk address or pronomen
    He grew incensed.
'Run, Ganymede!' quo I,
  'Stay me wi flagons!'
                    (Or maybe tappit-hens)
    —But I digress.
It was rum, I mynd the nou, rum was the bree,
Rum and draucht Bass.
                    —Sheer *hara-kiri!*

(iii)
—Ah, she was a bonnie cou!
Saxteen, maybe sevinteen, nae mair,
Her mither in attendance, *comme il faut*
Pour les jeunes filles bien élevées,
  Drinkan like a bluidie whaul tae!
Wee breists, round and ticht and fou
Like sweet Pomona in the oranger grove;
Her shanks were lang, but no ower lang, and plump,
  A lassie's shanks,
Wi the meisurance o Venus—
  Achteen inch the hoch frae heuchle-bane til knap,
  Achteen inch the cauf frae knap til cuit
As is the true perfectioun calculate
By the Auntients efter due regaird
For this and that,
                  The true meisurance
  O' the Venus dei Medici,
  The Aphrodite Anadyomene
And aa the goddesses o hie antiquitie—
  Siclike were the shanks and hochs
O' Sandra the cou o the auld Black Bull.
  Her een were, naiturallie, expressionless,
Blank as chuckie-stanes, like the bits
O' blae-green gless ye find by the sea.
                  —Nostalgia! Ah, sweet regrets!—

Her blee was yon o sweet sexteen,
Her lyre as white as Dian's chastitie
    In yon fyle, fousome, clartie slum.
Sound the tocsin, sound the drum!
The Haas o Balclutha ring wi revelrie!
The Prince sall dine at Hailie Rude the nicht!

(iv)
The lums o the reikan toun
Spreid aa ablow, and round
As far as ye coud leuk
The yalla squares o winnocks
Lit ilkane by a nakit yalla sterne
Blenkan, aff, syne on again,
Out and in and out again
As the thrang mercat throve,
    The haill toun at it
Aa the lichts pip-poppan
    In and out and in again
        I' the buts and bens
            And single ends,
                The banks and braes
    O' the toueran cliffs o lands,
Haill tenements, wards and burghs, counties,
    Regalities and jurisdictiouns,
        Continents and empires
            Gien ower entire
Til the joukerie-poukerie!
Hech, sirs, whatna feck of fockerie!
Shades o Knox, the hochmagandie!
    My bonie Edinburrie,
        Auld Skulduggerie!
Flat on her back sevin nichts o the week,
Earnan her breid wi her hurdies' sweit.

—And Dian's siller chastitie
Muved owre the reikan lums,
Biggan a ferlie toun o jet and ivorie
That was but blackened stane
Whar Bothwell rade and Huntly

132

And fair Montrose and aa the lave
Wi silken leddies doun til the grave.
   —The hoofs strak siller on the causie!
      And I mysel in cramasie!

(v)
There Sandra sleepan, like a doe shot
I' the midnicht wuid, wee paps
Like munes, mune-aipples gaithert
   I' the Isles o Youth,
Her flung straucht limbs
A paradisal archipelagie
Inhaudan divers bays, lagoons,
Great carses, strands and sounds,
Islands and straits, peninsulies,
   Whar traders, navigators,
    Odyssean gangrels, gubernators,
    Mutineers and maister-marineers,
And aa sic outland chiels micht utilise wi ease
Cheap flouered claiths and beads,
Gawds, wire and sheenan nails
   And siclike flichtmafletherie
In fair and just excambion
For aa the ferlies o the southren seas
That chirm in thy deep-dernit creeks,
    —My Helen douce as aipple-jack
      That cack't the bed in exstasie!
Ah, belle nostalgie de la boue!

—Sandra, princess-leman o a nicht o lust,
    That girdelt the fishie seas
     Frae Leith til Honolulu,
Maistress o the white mune Cytherean,
    Tak this bardic tribute nou!
Immortalitie sall croun thy heid wi bays,
   Laurel and rosemarie and rue!
You that spierit me nae questions,
   Spierit at me nocht,
    Acceptit me and teuk me in
    A guest o the hous, nae less;

Teuk aa there was to gie
　　　(And yon was peerie worth),
Gied what ye didna loss—
　　　A bien and dernit fleeman's-firth
　　　And bodie's easement
　　　And saft encomfortin!
O Manon! Marguerite! Camille!
　　　And maybe tae the pox—
　　　　　　Ach, weill!

forenent—over against　　　tine—forget　　biggit—built　　howffs—dens
auntient—ancient　　　speakin-til—addressing　　collieshangie—row
bree—brew　　hoch—thigh　　heuchle-bane—hip-bone　　knap—knee
cuit—ankle　　blee—complexion　　chiels—fellows　　ferlies—wonders
chirm—noise of waters rippling

HAMEWITH

'En ma fin est mon commencement.'
　　　　　　MARIE STUART

Man at the end
Til the womb wends,
Fisher til sea,
Hunter to hill,
Miner the pit seeks,
Sodjer the bield.

As bairn on breist
Seeks his first need
Makar his thocht prees,
Doer his deed,
Sanct his peace
And sinner remeid.

Man in dust is lain
And exile wins hame.

til—to　　　makar—poet　　prees—questions

BISEARTA

Chì mi rè geard na h-oidhche
dreòs air chrith 'na fhroidhneas thall air fàire,
ag clapail le a sgiathaibh,
a' sgapadh s ag ciaradh rionnagan na h-àird' ud.

Shaoileadh tu gu'n cluinnte,
ge cian, o 'bhuillsgein ochanaich no caoineadh
ràn corruich no gàir fuatha,
comhart chon cuthaitch uaith no ulfhairt fhaolchon,
gu'n ruigeadh drannd an fhòirneirt
o'n fhùirneis òmair iomall fhèin an tsaoghail;
ach sud a' dol an leud e
ri oir an speur an tosdachd olc is aognuidh.

C'ainm an nochd a th'orra,
na sràidean bochda anns an sgeith gach uinneag
a lasraichean s a deatach,
a sradagan is sgreadail a luchd thuinidh,
is taigh air thaigh 'ga reubadh
am broinn a chéile am brùchdadh toit' a' tuiteam?
Is có an nochd tha 'g atach
am Bàs a theachd gu grad 'nan cainntibh uile,
no a' spàirn measg chlach is shailthean
air bhàinidh ag gairm air cobhair, is nach cluinnear?
Có an nochd a phàigheas
sean chis àbhaisteach na fala cumant?

Uair dearg mar lod na h-àraich,
uair bàn mar ghile thràighte an eagail éitigh,
a' dìreadh s uair a' teàrnadh,
a' sineadh le sitheadh àrd s ag call a mheudachd,
a' fannachadh car aitil
a ag at mar anail dhiabhuil air dhéinead,
an t-Olc 'na chridhe a 'na chuisle,
chì mi 'na bhuillean a' sìoladh s a' leum e.
Tha'n dreòs 'na oillt air fàire,

'na fhàinne ròis is òir am bun nan speuran,
a' breugnachadh s ag àicheadh
le 'shoillse sèimhe àrsaidh àrd nan reultan.

BIZERTA
from the Gaelic of George Campbell Hay
(Scots version by Hugh MacDiarmid)

While I'm standin' guard the nicht I see
Awa' doon yonder on the laich skyline
A restless lowe, beatin' its wings and scatterin' and
    dimmin'
A' the starns abune wi'-in reach o' its shine.

You'd think, tho' it's hine awa', there 'ud be heard
Wailin' and lamentation pourin' oot frae't,
That roarin' and screamin', and the yowlin' o' mad dogs,
'Ud come frae that amber furnace a' the noises o' fear
    and hate,
And flood the haill lift—insteed o' which the foul glare
Juist rises and fa's alang the horizon in ghastly silence there.

What are the names the nicht o' thae puir streets
Whaur ilka lozen belches flame and soot and the screams
    o' the folk
As hoose eftir hoose is rent and caves in in a blash o' smoke?

And whase are the voices cryin' on Daith the nicht
In sae mony different tongues to come quick and end
    their plight
Or screamin' in frenzy for help and no' heard, hid
Under yon muckle heaps o' burnin' stanes and beams,
And payin' there the auld accustomed tax o' common
    bluid?

Noo reid like a battlefield puddle, noo wan
Like the dirty pallor o' fear, shootin' up and syne
Sinkin' again, I see Evil like a hammerin' pulse or the
    spasms

136

O' a hert in the deidthraw aye rax up and dwine
The fitfu' fire, a horror on the horizon, a ring
O' rose and gowd at the fit o' the lift belies and denies
The ancient hie beauty and peace o' the starns themselves
As its foul glare crines and swells.

AN SEALGAIR AGUS AN AOIS

Cuing mo dhroma an aois a nis,
   rib mo choise, robach, liath:
fear thig eadar soills' is sùilean,
   fear thig eadar rùn is gnìomh.

Fàgaidh e am faillean crotach,
   ris gach dos 's e chuireas sgian:
is, och, b'e 'm bàrr air gach miosguinn
   tighinn eadar mi's an sliabh.

Thug e dhìom a' Chruach Chaorainn,
   's an gunna caol, 's an ealchainn shuas:
bhuin e dhiom mo neart, am meàirleach,
   dh'fhàg a mi gun làmh, gun luaths,

Na'n robh aige corp a ghlacainn,
   's na'n tachrainn ris leis fhéin 's a' bheinn,
bhiodh saltairt ann is fraoch 'ga reubadh,
   's fuil air feur mu'n sgaradh sinn.

THE AULD HUNTER
from the Gaelic of George Campbell Hay
(Scots version by Hugh MacDiarmid)

Eild comes owre me like a yoke on my craig,
A girn roon' my feet, the lourd and the chill.
Betwixt my sicht and the licht it comes,
It comes betwixt the deed and the will.

This is the thing that warps the sapling
And sets its knife to the aipple's root,
But the warst deed o' a' its spite has been
To filch the hill frae under my foot.

My narrow gun and the paths o' the cruach
Eild has stown, wha's deef and heeds nae grief;
My hand and my foot, this Blear-eyed's stown them
And a' my cheer, like a hertless thief.

But gin Eild were a man that hauns could grapple
And I could come on him secretly
Up there on the hill when naebody passes
Certes! Grass 'ud be trampled or he gat free!

STILL GYTE, MAN?

'Still gyte, man? Stude I in yere claes
I'd thole nae beggar's nichts an' days,
chap-chappan, whidderan lik a moose,
at ae same cauld an' steekit hoose?

'What stane has she tae draw yere een?
What gars ye, syne she aye has been
as toom an' hertless as a hoor,
gang sornan kindness at her dure?'

'Though ye should talk a hunner year,
the windblawn wave will seek the shore,
the muirlan watter seek the sea.
Then, wheesht man. Sae it is wi me.'

THE OLD FISHERMAN

Greet the bights that gave me shelter,
they will hide me no more with the horns of their forelands
I peer in a haze, my back is stooping;
my dancing days for fishing are over.

138

The shoot that was straight in the wood withers,
the bracken shrinks red in the rain and shrivels,
the eyes that would gaze in the sun waver;
my dancing days for fishing are over.

The old boat must seek the shingle,
her wasting side hollow the gravel,
the hand that shakes must leave the tiller;
my dancing days for fishing are over.

The sea was good night and morning,
the winds were friends, the calm was kindly—
the snow seeks the burn, the brown fronds scatter;
my dancing days for fishing are over.

W.S. GRAHAM

THE NIGHTFISHING

I

Very gently struck
The quay night bell.

Now within the dead
Of night and the dead
Of my life I hear
My name called from far out.
I'm come to this place
(Come to this place)
Which I'll not pass
Though one shall pass
Wearing seemingly
This look I move as
This staring second
Breaks my home away
Through always every
Night through every whisper
From the first that once
Named me to the bone.
Yet this place finds me

And forms itself again.
This present place found me.

Owls from the land.
Gulls cry from the water.
And that wind honing
The roof-ridge is out of
Nine hours west on the main
Ground with likely a full
Gale unwinding it.

Gently the quay bell
Strikes the held air.
Strikes the held air like
Opening a door
So that all the dead
Brought to harmony
Speak out on silence.

I bent to the lamp. I cupped
My hand to the glass chimney.
Yet it was a stranger's breath
From out of my mouth that
Shed the light. I turned out
Into the salt dark
And turned my collar up.

And now again almost
Blindfold with the bright
Hemisphere unprised
Ancient overhead,
I am befriended by
This sea which utters me.

The hull slewed out through
The lucky turn and trembled
Under way then. The twin
Screws spun sweetly alive
Spinning position away.

Far out faintly calls
The continual sea.

Now within the dead
Of night and the dead
Of all my life I go.
I'm one ahead of them
Turned in below.
I'm borne, in their eyes,
Through the staring world.

The present opens its arms.

from III

We are at the hauling then hoping for it
The hard slow haul of a net white with herring
Meshed hard. I haul, using the boat's cross-heave
We've started, holding fast as we rock back,
Taking slack as we go to. The day rises brighter
Over us and the gulls rise in a wailing scare
From the nearest net-floats. And the unfolding water
Mingles its dead.

Now better white I can say what's better sighted,
The white net flashing under the watched water,
The near net dragging back with the full belly
Of a good take certain, so drifted easy
Slow down on us or us hauled up upon it
Curved in a garment down to thicker fathoms.
The hauling nets come in sawing the gunwale
With herring scales.

The air bunches to a wind and roused sea-cries.
The weather moves and stoops high over us and
There the forked tern, where my look's whetted on
    distance,
Quarters its hunting sea. I haul slowly
Inboard the drowning flood as into memory,
Braced at the breathside in my net of nerves.

We haul and drift them home. The winds slowly
Turn round on us and

Gather towards us with dragging weights of water
Sleekly swelling across the humming sea
And gather heavier. We haul and hold and haul
Well the bright chirpers home, so drifted whitely
All a blinding garment out of the grey water.
And, hauling hard in the drag, the nets come in,
The headrope a sore pull and feeding its brine
Into our hacked hands.

Over the gunwale over into our deep lap
The herring come in, staring from their scales,
Fruitful as our deserts would have it out of
The deep and shifting seams of water. We haul
Against time fallen ill over the gathering
Rush of the sea together. The calms dive down.
The strident kingforked airs roar in their shell.
We haul the last

Net home and the last tether off the gathering
Run of the started sea. And then was the first
Hand at last lifted getting us swung against
Into the homing quarter, running that white grace
That sails me surely ever away from home.
And we hold into it as it moves down on
Us running white on the hull heeled to light.
Our bow heads home

Into the running blackbacks soaring us loud
High up in open arms of the towering sea.
The steep bow heaves, hung on these words, towards
What words your lonely breath blows out to meet it.
It is the skilled keel itself knowing its own
Fathoms it further moves through, with us there
Kept in its common timbers, yet each of us
Unwound upon

By a lonely behaviour of the all common ocean.
I cried headlong from my dead. The long rollers,
Quick on the crests and shirred with fine foam,
Surge down then sledge their green tons weighing dead
Down on the shuddered deck-boards. And shook off
All that white arrival upon us back to falter
Into the waking spoil and to be lost in
The mingling world.

So we were started back over that sea we
Had worked widely all fish-seasons and over
Its shifting grounds, yet now risen up into
Such humours, I felt like a farmer tricked to sea.
For it sailed sore against us. It grew up
To black banks that crossed us. It stooped, beaked..
Its brine burnt us. I was chosen and given.
It rose as risen

Treachery becomes myself, to clip me amorously
Off from all common breath. Those fires burned
Sprigs of the foam and branching tines of water.
It rose so white, soaring slowly, up
On us, then broke, down on us. It became a mull
Against our going and unfastened under us and
Curdled from the stern. It shipped us at each blow.
The brute weight

Of the living sea wrought us, yet the boat sleeked lean
Into it, upheld by the whole sea-brunt heaved,
And hung on the swivelling tops. The tiller raised
The siding tide to wrench us and took a good
Ready hand to hold it. Yet we made a seaway
And minded all the gear was fast, and took
Our spell at steering. And we went keeled over
The streaming sea.

See how, like an early self, it's loath to leave
And stares from the scuppers as it swirls away
To be clenched up. What a great width stretches
Farsighted away fighting in its white straits

On either bow, but bears up our boat on all
Its plaiting strands. This wedge driven in
To the twisting water, we rode. The bow shores
The long rollers.

The keel climbs and, with screws spinning out of their bite,
We drive down into the roar of the great doorways,
Each time almost to overstay, but start
Up into again the yelling gale and hailing
Shot of the spray. Yet we should have land
Soon marking us out of this thick distance and
How far we're in. Who is that poor sea-scholar,
Braced in his hero,

Lost in his book of storms there? It is myself.
So he who died is announced. This mingling element
Gives up myself. Words travel from what they once
Passed silence with. Here, in this intricate death,
He goes as fixed on silence as ever he'll be.
Leave him, nor cup a hand to shout him out
Of that, his home. Or, if you would, O surely
There is no word,

There is not any to go over that.
It is now as always this difficult air
We look towards each other through. And is there
Some singing look or word or gesture of grace
Or naked wide regard from the encountered face,
Goes ever true through the difficult air?
Each word speaks its own speaker to his death.
And we saw land

At last marked on the tenting mist and we could
Just make out the ridge running from the north
To the Black Rosses, and even mark the dark hint
Of Skeer well starboard. Now inside the bight
The sea was loosening and the screws spun steadier
Beneath us. We still shipped the blown water but
It broke white, not green weight caved in on us.
In out of all

That forming and breaking sea we came on the long
Swell close at last inshore with the day grey
With mewing distances and mist. The rocks rose
Waving their lazy friendly weed. We came in
Moving now by the world's side. And O the land lay
Just as we knew it well all along that shore
Akin to us with each of its dear seamarks. And lay
Like a mother.

We came in, riding steady in the bay water,
A sailing pillar of gulls, past the cockle strand.
And springing teal came out off the long sand. We
Moved under the soaring land sheathed in fair water
In that time's morning grace. I uttered that place
And left each word I was. The quay-heads lift up
To pass us in. These sea-worked measures end now.
And this element

Ends as we move off from its formal instant.
Now he who takes my place continually anew
Speaks me thoroughly perished into another.
And the quay opened its arms. I heard the sea
Close on him gently swinging on oiled hinges.
Moored here, we cut the motor quiet. He that
I'm not lies down. Men shout. Words break. I am
My fruitful share.

LETTER II

Burned in this element
To the bare bone, I am
Trusted on the language.
I am to walk to you
Through the night and through
Each word you make between
Each word I burn bright in
On this wide reach. And you,
Within what arms you lie,
Hear my burning ways

Across these darknesses
That move and merge like foam.
Lie in the world's room,
My dear, and contribute
Here where all dialogues write.

Younger in the towered
Tenement of night he heard
The shipyards with nightshifts
Of lathes turning their shafts.
His voice was a humble ear
Hardly turned to her.
Then in a welding flash
He found his poetry arm
And turned the coat of his trade.
From where I am I hear
Clearly his heart beat over
Clydeside's far hammers
And the nightshipping firth.
What's he to me? Only
Myself I died from into
These present words that move.
In that high tenement
I got a great grave.

Tonight in sadly need
Of you I move inhuman
Across this space of dread
And silence in my mind.
I walk the dead water
Burning language towards
You where you lie in the dark
Ascension of all words.
Yet where? Where do you lie
Lost to my cry and hidden
Away from the world's downfall?
O offer some way tonight
To make your love take place
In every word. Reply.
Time's branches burn to hear.

146

Take heed. Reply. Here
I am driven burning on
This loneliest element. Break
Break me out of this night,
This silence where you are not,
Nor any within earshot.
Break break me from this high
Helmet of idiocy.
Water water wallflower
Growing up so high
We are all children
We all must die.
Except Willie Graham
The fairest of them all.
He can dance and he can sing
And he can turn his face to the wall.
Fie, fie, fie for shame
Turn your face to the wall again.

Yes laugh then cloudily laugh
Though he sat there as deaf
And worn to a stop
As the word had given him up.
Stay still. That was the sounding
Sea he moved on burning
His still unending cry.
That night hammered and waved
Its starry shipyard arms,
And it came to inherit
His death where these words merge.
This is his night writ large.
In Greenock the bright breath
Of night's array shone forth
On the nightshifting town.
Thus younger burning in
The best of his puny gear
He early set out
To write him to this death
And to that great breath
Taking of the sea,

The graith of Poetry.

My musing love lie down
Within his arms. He dies
Word by each word into

Myself now at this last
Word I die in. This last.

TOM SCOTT

AULD SANCT-AUNDRIANS—BRAND THE BUILDER

On winter days, about the gloamin hour,
Whan the knock on the college touer
Is chappan lowsin-time,
And ilka mason packs his mell and tools awa
Ablow his banker, and bien forenenst the waa
The labourer haps the lave o the lime
Wi soppan secks, to keep it frae a frost, or faa
O suddent snaw
Duran the nicht,
And scrawnie craws flap in the shell-green licht
Towards yon bane-bare rickle o trees
That heeze
Up on the knowe abuin the toun,
And the red goun
Is happan mony a student frae the snell nor-easter,
Malcolm Brand, the maister,
Seean the last hand thru the yett
Afore he bars and padlocks it,
Taks ae look round his stourie yaird
Whaur chunks o stane are liggan
Like the ruins o some auld-farrant biggin:
Picks a skelf out o his beard,
Scliffs his tackey buits and syne
Clunters hamelins doun the wyn'.

Alang the shore,
The grienan white sea-owsen ramp and roar.

148

MAURICE LINDSAY

AT HANS CHRISTIAN ANDERSEN'S BIRTHPLACE, ODENSE, DENMARK

Sunlight folds back pages of quiet shadows
against the whitewashed walls of his birthplace.
   Tourists move
through crowded antiseptic rooms and ponder
what row after row of glass-cased papers ought to prove.

Somehow the long-nosed gangling boy who was only
at home in fairyland, has left no clues.
The tinder-box of Time we rub
answers us each way we choose.

For kings have now no daughters left for prizes.
Swineherds must remain swineherds; and no spell
can make the good man prince; psychiatrists
have dredged up wonder from the wishing well.

The whole of his terrible, tiny world might be
dismissed as a beautiful madman's dream, but that each
   of us knows
whenever we move out from the warmth of our loneliness
we may be wearing the Emperor's new clothes.

AT THE MOUTH OF THE ARDYNE

The water rubs against itself,
glancing many faces at me.
One winces as the dropped fly
tears its tension. Then it heals.

Being torn doesn't matter.
The water just goes on saying
all that water has to say,
what the dead come back to.

151

Then a scar opens.
Something of water is ripped out,
a struggle with swung air.
I batter it on a loaf of stone.

The water turns passing faces,
innumerable pieces of silver.
I wash my hands, pack up, and
go home wishing I hadn't come.

Later, I eat my guilt.

A BALLAD OF ORPHEUS

On the third day after her unexpected death,
Orpheus descended into Hell.
It wasn't hard to find. He knew the directions well;
asleep, he'd often read them by the light of his own breath.

The doorkeeper was surly, but let him in;
he had no reason to keep anyone out.
Glaring like a lit city, a kind of visible shout
fungused about the place, an absolute din

of all notes, overtones and unheard sounds at once.
To keep his sense of self intact, he struck
a few familiar chords, and as his luck
would have it, she, who all along had felt a hunch

something unusual would happen, heard the order
and limiting purpose of his playing; and being not yet
fully subtracted out of herself to fit
Hell's edgeless ambiguities, broke from the border

of blurring dissolution, and moved towards her lover
as a cloud might move in the world of gods above.
He guessed that shape and stir to be his love
Eurydice, well knowing that no other

idea of woman would answer to the lyre
that sang against his loins. She came to him crying
aloud her numbed womanly tenderness, trying
to warm her cold half-body at the core of his fire.

But without a word said, he seized her hand
and began pulling her roughly along the road,
past the doorkeeper, who smirked, seeing the load
he carried. She, being woman, couldn't understand

that love in action needs no drag of speech,
and pled with him to turn round once and kiss
her. Of all the conditions the gods had imposed, this
was the one he dared not disobey. Reproach

followed reproach; till, as he fled
through shadow to shadow, suddenly it seemed
that the only absolute good was what he'd dreamed
of her. So Orpheus stopped, and slowly turned his head.

At once she began to small. He watched her disappear
backwards from him, and thought it best
that things should be so. How could he have stood the test
of constant loving, always with the fear

of his first loss ahead of him again,
believing happiness ends in boredom or pain?
So Orpheus returned by the same lane
as he went down by, to compose himself in a world of men.

AN ELEGY
(Matthew Lindsay: 1884-1969)

You might have died so many kinds of death
as you drove yourself through eighty-four Novembers—

1916. The Cameronian officer
keeping the Lewis gun he commanded chattering
over the seething mud, that the enemy

153

should be told only in terms of bulky bodies,
for which, oak leaves, a mention in dispatches.

1918. The fragment of a shell
leaving one side of a jaw and no speech,
the bone graft from the hip. Shakespeare mouthed
(most of the others asserting silences)
over and over again, till the old words
shaped themselves into audibility.

1921. An eighty-per-cent
disability pension, fifty the limit of life
expectancy, a determination of courage
that framed the public man, the ready maker
of witty dinner speeches, the League of Nations,
the benefits of insurance, the private man
shut in his nightly study, unapproachable,
sufficient leader of sporting tournaments,
debates, and the placing of goodwill greetings in clubs.

1935. Now safely past
the doctors' prophecies. Four children, a popular
outward man wearing maturity,
top of his business tree, when the sap falters
and the soon-to-be again confounded doctors
pronounce a world-wide cruise the only hope,
not knowing hope was all he ever needed
or counted on to have to reckon with.

1940-50. Wartime fears
not for himself but for his family,
the public disappointments and the private
disasters written off with stock quotations
from Shakespeare or Fitzgerald, perhaps to prove
the well-known commonness of experience,
the enemy across the mud, old age.

1959. It was necessary
at seventy-five, to show he couldn't be taken
by enfilading weaknesses. A horse

raised his defiance up. It threw him merely
to Russia on a stretcher, with two sticks
to lean beginner's Russian upon.

1969. The end of a decade
of surgeons, paling blindness, heart attacks
all beaten with familiar literature
bent into philosophic platitudes,
to the January day in his dressing-gown
when he sat recording plans for a last Burns Supper—

You might have died so many kinds of death
as you drove yourself through eighty-four Novembers
till you fell from your bed, apologized for such foolishness,
and from your sleep rode out where no man goes.

AN INVERNESS HOTEL

Outside the restless window of my sleep
seagulls rip aside the dawn's caul.
I stagger through to life, pull back the curtains
and watch them scissoring the mottled scraps
of yesterday's discarded human refuse
that waits for shuffling binmen to remove.

Snap-hunting amateur photographers
fall for them every time; puffily folded,
winking on rusty bollards; in the wake
of churning ships, quick dips of wing, long glides
that boast them masters of their element;
or dropping streaks, white as themselves, on decks,
abandoned quays or fresh-ploughed coastal fields.

It is, perhaps, their dazzling isolation
that fascinates us, smooth in company;
the rocks they breed on inaccessible,
the death they die an unaccountable plunge
seawards; lonely and final as a plane,
into whose jets they sometimes blunder, tumbles,

155

a vanished blob gone off a radar screen
that signals for a while our brief concern.

Seagulls leave no trace of their own wreckage.

THE GIRL FROM NEWTON MEARNS

O Lord, since Thou omnipotently knowest
all that occurs within Thy servant's heart;
and since whatever things are there, Thou sowest,
of blame Thou'llt surely take a little part.
Last Wednesday, as down the street I goest,
I saw a woman looking much more smart
yet wearing just the same as me. Ah woest!
Pretending but to stumble, with a smart
kick from my heel, she, falling, overthrowest
a vendor's fruit and vegetable cart.
The man, without Thy sense of quid pro quoest,
then called me, Lord a careless fuckan tart!
Forgive me, Lord, though he was not the beauest . . .
somehow I had to pay Thy debt I owest.

TOWARD LIGHT

The distant fog-horns bicker, the near ones boom;
light bats across the ceiling of the room
where, forty years ago, I watched, awake;
a still unfocused schoolboy out to take
life by the meaning. Then, the mist that gripped
the perfumed garden, kept the sea tight-lipped,
hung vague on sheltering curtains; the boy's mind
compassed on ships whose fogs lay far behind.
Now, with the frame loose, the window bare,
a blunt beam's thrown back on its own stare.

HAMISH HENDERSON

FROM ELEGIES FOR THE DEAD IN CYRENAICA

First Elegy, End of a Campaign

There are many dead in the brutish desert, who lie uneasy
among the scrub in this landscape of half-wit
stunted ill-will. For the dead land is insatiate
and necrophilous. The sand is blowing about still.
Many who for various reasons, or because of mere
    unanswerable compulsion, came here
and fought among the clutching gravestones, shivered and
    sweated,
cried out, suffered thirst, were stoically silent, cursed
the spittering machine-guns, were homesick for Europe
and fast embedded in quicksand of Africa agonized and
    died.
And sleep now. Sleep here the sleep of the dust.

There were our own, there were the others.
Their deaths were like their lives, human and animal.
There were no gods and precious few heroes.
What they regretted when they died had nothing to do
    with race and leader, realm indivisible,
laboured Augustan speeches or vague imperial heritage.
(They saw through that guff before the axe fell.) Their
    longing turned to
the lost world glimpsed in the memory of letters:
an evening at the pictures in the friendly dark,
two knowing conspirators smiling and whispering secrets;
    or else
a family gathering in the homely kitchen
with Mum so proud of her boys in uniform: their
    thoughts trembled
between moments of estrangement, and ecstatic moments
of reconciliation: and their desire
crucified itself against the unutterable shadow of someone
whose photo was in their wallets.
Then death made his incision.

There were our own, there were the others.
Therefore, minding the great word of Glencoe's
son, that we should not disfigure ourselves
with villainy of hatred; and seeing that all
have gone down like curs into anonymous silence,
I will bear witness for I knew the others.
Seeing that littoral and interior are alike indifferent
and the birds are drawn again to our welcoming north
why should I not sing *them*, the dead, the innocent?

Third Elegy, Leaving the City

Morning After. Get moving. Cheerio. Be seeing you
when this party's over. Right, driver, get weaving.

The truck pulls out
along the corniche. We dismiss with the terseness
of a newsreel the casino and the column,
the scrofulous sellers of obscenity,
the garries, the girls and the preposterous skyline.

Leave them. And out past the stinking tanneries,
the maritime Greek cafes, the wogs and the nets
drying among seaweed. Through the periphery of the city
itching under flagrant sunshine. Faster. We are nearing
the stretch leading to the salt-lake Mareotis.
Sand now, and dust-choked fig-trees. This is the road
where convoys are ordered to act in case of ambush.
A straight run through now to the coastal sector.
One sudden thought wounds: it's a half-hour or over
since we saw the last skirt. And for a moment we regret
the women, and the harbour with a curve so perfect
it seems it was drawn with the mouseion's protractor.

Past red-rimmed eye of the salt-lake. So long then,
holy filth of the living. We are going to the familiar
filth of your negation, to rejoin the proletariat
of levelling death. Stripes are shed and ranks levelled
in death's proletariat. There the Colonel of Hussars,

158

the keen Sapper Subaltern with a first in economics
and the sergeant well known in international football
crouch with Jock and Jame in their holes like helots.
Distinctions become vain, the former privileges quite
     pointless
in that new situation. See our own and the opponents
advance, meet and merge: the commingled columns
lock, strain, disengage and join issue with the dust.

Do not regret
that we have still in history to suffer
or comrade that we are the agents
of a dialectic that can destroy us
but like a man prepared, like a brave man
bid farewell to the city, and quickly
move forward on the road leading west by the salt-lake.
Like a man for long prepared, like a brave man,
like to the man who was worthy of such a city
be glad that the case admits no other solution,
acknowledge with pride the clear imperative of action
and bid farewell to her, to Alexandria, whom you are losing.

And these, advancing from the direction of Sollum,
swaddies in tropical kit, lifted in familiar vehicles
are they mirage—ourselves out of a mirror?
No, they too, leaving the plateau of Marmarica
for the serpentine of the pass, they advancing towards us
along the coast road, are the others, the brothers
in death's proletariat, they are our victims and betrayers
advancing by the seashore to the same assignation.
We send them our greetings out of the mirror.

ALEXANDER SCOTT

RECIPE: TO MAK A BALLANT

To mak a ballant:
tak onie image sclents frae the dark o your mind,
sieve it through twal years' skill
i the fewest words can haud it
(meantime steeran in your hert's bluid),

159

spice wi wit, saut wi passion,
bile i the hettest fire your love can kindle,
and serve at the scaud in your strangmaist stanza
(the haill process aa to be dune at aince)

Syne rin like hell afore the result explodes!

SCRIEVIN

I walkit air, I walkit late
By craigs o gloamin-coloured stane,
I heard the sea-maws skirl and keen
Like sclate-pens scraichan ower a sclate.

I walkit late, I walkit air
By parks that winter smairged wi snaw,
I saw the spoor o pad and claw
Like ink on paper mirkened there.

I lippened syne, I lookit syne,
But cudna richt jalouse ava
A word o what I heard or saw
Scrievit by hands sae unlike mine.

HAAR IN PRINCES STREET

The heicht o the biggins is happit in rauchens o haar,
    The statues alane
  Stand clearly, heid til fit in stane,
And lour frae *then* and *thonder* at *hencefurth* and *here*.

The past on pedestals, girnan frae ilka feature,
    Wi granite frouns
  They glower at the present's feckless loons,
Its gangrels tint i the haar that fankles the future.

The fowk o flesh, stravaigan wha kens whither,
    And come frae whar,
  Hudder like ghaists i the gastrous haar,
Forfochten and wae i the smochteran smore o the weather.

They swaiver and flirn i the freeth like straes i the sea,
    An airtless swither,
  Steeran awa the t'ane frae t'ither,
Alane, and lawlie aye to be lanesome sae.

But heich i the lift (whar the haar is skailan fairlie
    In blufferts o wind)
  And blacker nor nicht whan starns are blind,
The Castle looms, a fell, a fabulous ferlie.

Dragonish, darksome, dourlie grapplan the Rock
    Wi claws o stane
  That scart our historie bare til the bane,
It braks like Fate throu Time's wanchancy reek.

haar—mist   heicht—height   biggins—buildings   happit—covered
rauchens—mantles   heid til fit—head to foot   thonder—yonder
girnan—grimacing   ilka—every   frouns—frowns   feckless—incapable
loons—boys   gangrels—tramps, wanderers   tint—lost   fankles—
entangles   fowk—folk   stravaigan—wandering   whar—where
hudder—huddle   ghaists—ghosts   gastrous—monstrous   for-
fochten—tired out   wae—sad   smochteran—smothering   smore—
suffocation   swaiver—totter   flirn—twist   freeth—foam   straes—
straws   airtless—without direction   t'ane frae t'ither—the one from
the other   lawlie—loath   lanesome—lonely   sae—so   lift—sky
skailan—dispersing   fairlie—in good measure   blufferts—gusts
nicht—night   starns—stars   fell—terrible   ferlie—wonder   scart—
scratch   wanchancy—evil-boding   reek—smoke

CONTINENT O VENUS

  She lies ablow my body's lust and love,
  A country dearly-kent, and yet sae fremd

That she's at aince thon Tir-nan-Og I've dreamed,
The airt I've lived in, whar I mean to live,
And mair, much mair, a mixter-maxter warld
Whar fact and dream are taigled up and snorled.
I ken ilk bay o aa her body's strand,
Yet ken them new ilk time I come to shore,
For she's the uncharted sea whar I maun fare
To find anither undiscovered land,
To find it fremd, and yet to find it dear,
To seek it aye, and aye be bydan there.

dearly-kent—dearly-known   fremd—strange   Tir-nan-Og—land of
youth   airt—place   mair—more   mixter-maxter—mixed up
taigled—entangled   snorled—knotted   ken—know   maun—must
bydan—staying

POEM BEFORE BIRTH

She carries life in her body
as a girl in a dry country carries
a pitcher of water cupped in her hands
delighting
the thirsty eyes of the dwellers
in those parched lands.

She is as quiet and as certain
as Earth in reluctant spring
which waits for a night of warm showers
dissolving
the last delay of winter
and dazzling the dawn with flowers.

SABBATH

Come unto me, all ye that are heavy-laden

The portly paunches trundled
the few short steps (O merciful religion!)
from the car to the door of the kirk,
the loaded furs lurching
from limousines to cushioned pews.

Pagan, I paused,
the Sunday papers under my infidel arm,
amazed at the joyful vision of
gentle Jesus
kicking camel-fat backsides
through a needle's eye.

CRY

Breakdown, breakdown, lay me low,
I'll go where all the furies go,
Into my own Orestian heart,
And tear it apart, tear it apart.

Breakdown, breakdown, hoist me high,
I'll fly where all the vultures fly,
Into my own Orphean brain,
And pick it clean, pick it clean.

Breakdown, breakdown, drive me deep,
I'll creep where all the blindworms creep,
Into my own Tiresian blood,
And drink its flood, drink its flood.

Breakdown, breakdown, pay me peace,
I'll cease where all the madmen cease,
Inside my own Oedipan mind,
And brand it blind, brand it blind.

BALLADE OF BEAUTIES

Miss Israel Nineteen-Sixty-Eight is new,
A fresh-poured form her swimsuit moulds to sleekness,
Legs long, breasts high, the shoulders firm and true,
The waist a lily wand without a weakness,
The hair, *en brosse* and black, is shorn to bleakness,
Yet shines as stars can make the midnight do—
But still my mind recalls more maiden meekness,
Miss Warsaw Ghetto Nineteen-Forty-Two.

Her masters filmed her kneeling stripped to sue
The mercy barred as mere unmanning weakness,
Or raking rubbish-dumps for crusts to chew,
Or licking boots to prove her slavish meekness,
Or baring loins to lie beneath the bleakness
Of conqueror's lust (and forced to smile it through),
Her starving flesh a spoil preferred to sleekness,
Miss Warsaw Ghetto Nineteen-Forty-Two.

The prize she won was given not to few
But countless thousands, paid the price of meekness,
And paid in full, with far too high a due,
By sadist dreams transformed to functioned sleekness,
A pervert prophet's weakling hate of weakness
Constructing a mad machine that seized and slew,
The grave her last reward, the final bleakness,
Miss Warsaw Ghetto Nineteen-Forty-Two.

Princesses, pale in death or sunned in sleekness,
I dedicate these loving lines to you,
Miss Israel Sixty-Eight and (murdered meekness)
Miss Warsaw Ghetto Nineteen-Forty-Two.

STEEL ON STANE

'Ingabeorg is the brawest o wemen'
—Sae it's scrievit i the Orkney tomb,
An aix the pen, the page a boulder,
Letters runic, hyne frae Rome.

Vikings reivit the tomb for treisure,
Fand there only a rickle o bane,
Yet some that socht i the deidly chaumer
Scarted thon lifey words on stane.

Nou they're deid themsels, the reivers,
Laid awa in loveless lairs
Or brunt wi their boats on widowan watters,
Sunk the greed for sillar and glory.

164

Gane the greed for gowd and glory
Drave them to doom as sodgers and seamen,
Yet steel on stane aye stobs like passion—
'Ingabeorg is the brawest o wemen.'

FROM 'SCOTCHED'

Scotch God
Kent His
Faither.

Scotch Religion
Damn
Aa.

Scotch Equality
Kaa the feet frae
Thon big bastard.

Scotch Optimism
Through a gless,
Darkly.

Scotch Pessimism
Nae
Gless.

Scotch Sex
In atween
Drinks.

Scotch Passion
Forgot
Mysel.

Scotch Free-love
Canna be
Worth much.

165

Scotch Lovebirds
Cheap
Cheep.

Scotch Education
I tellt ye
I tellt ye.

EDWIN MORGAN

KING BILLY

Grey over Riddrie the clouds piled up,
dragged their rain through the cemetery trees.
The gates shone cold. Wind rose
flaring the hissing leaves, the branches
swung, heavy, across the lamps.
Gravestones huddled in drizzling shadow,
flickering streetlights scanned the requiescats,
a name and an urn, a date, a dove
picked out, lost, half regained.
What is this dripping wreath, blown from its grave
red, white, blue, and gold
'To Our Leader of Thirty Years Ago'—

Bareheaded, in dark suits, with flutes
and drums, they brought him here, in procession
seriously, King Billy of Brigton, dead,
from Bridgeton Cross: a memory of violence,
brooding days of empty bellies,
billiard smoke and a sour pint,
boots or fists, famous sherrickings,
the word, the scuffle, the flash, the shout,
bloody crumpling in the close,
bricks for papish widows, get
the Conks next time, the Conks ambush
the Billy Boys, the Billy Boys the Conks till
Sillitoe scuffs the razors down the stank—
No, but it isn't the violence they remember
but the legend of a violent man
born poor, gang-leader in the bad times

of idleness and boredom, lost in better days,
a bouncer in a betting club,
a quiet man at last, dying
alone in Bridgeton in a box bed.
So a thousand people stopped the traffic
for the hearse of a folk hero and the flutes
threw 'Onward Christian Soldiers' to the winds
from unironic lips, the mourners kept
in step, and there were some who wept.

Go from the grave. The shrill flutes
are silent, the march dispersed.
Deplore what is to be deplored,
and then find out the rest.

GOOD FRIDAY

Three o'clock. The bus lurches
round into the sun. 'D's this go—'
he flops beside me—'right along Bath Street?
—Oh tha's, tha's all right, see I've
got to get some Easter eggs for the kiddies.
I've had a wee drink, ye understand—
ye'll maybe think it's a—funny day
to be celebratin—well, no but ye see
I wasny workin—I don't say it's right
I'm no sayin it's right, ye understand—ye understand?
But anyway tha's the way I look at it—
I'm no borin you, eh?—ye see today,
take today, I don't know what today's in aid of,
whether Christ was —crucified or was he—
rose fae the dead like, see what I mean?
You're an educatit man, you can tell me—
—Aye, well. There ye are. It's been seen
time and again, the workin man
has nae education, he jist canny—jist
hasny got it, know what I mean,
he's jist bliddy ignorant—Christ aye,
bliddy ignorant. Well—' The bus brakes violently,

he lunges for the stair, swings down—off,
into the sun for his Easter eggs,
on very
           nearly
                   steady
                           legs.

FROM GLASGOW SONNETS

A mean wind wanders through the backcourt trash.
Hackles on puddles rise, old mattresses
puff briefly and subside. Play-fortresses
of brick and bric-à-brac spill out some ash.
Four storeys have no windows left to smash,
but in the fifth a chipped sill buttresses
mother and daughter the last mistresses
of that black block condemned to stand, not crash.
Around them the cracks deepen, the rats crawl.
The kettle whimpers on a crazy hob.
Roses of mould grow from ceiling to wall.
The man lies late since he has lost his job,
smokes on one elbow, letting his coughs fall
thinly into an air too poor to rob.

DEATH IN DUKE STREET

A huddle on the greasy street—
cars stop, nose past, withdraw—
dull glint on soles of tackety boots,
frayed rough blue trousers, nondescript coat
stretching back, head supported
in strangers' arms, a crowd collecting—
'Whit's wrang?' 'Can ye see'm?'
'An auld fella, he's had it.'
On one side, a young mother in a headscarf
is kneeling to comfort him, her three-year-old son
stands puzzled, touching her coat, her shopping-bag
spills its packages that people look at

168

as they look at everything. On the other side
a youth, nervous, awkwardly now
at the centre of attention as he shifts his arm
on the old man's shoulders, wondering
what to say to him, glancing up at the crowd.
These were next to him when he fell,
and must support him into death.
He seems not to be in pain,
he is speaking slowly and quietly
but he does not look at any of them,
his eyes are fixed on the sky,
already he is moving out
beyond everything belonging.
As if he still belonged
they hold him very tight.

Only the hungry ambulance
howls for him through the staring squares.

NIGHT PILLION

Eleven struck. The traffic lights were green.
The shuddering machine let out its roar
As we sprang forward into brilliant streets.
Beyond your shoulders and helmet the walls rose
Well into darkness, mounted up, plunged past—
Hunting the clouds that hunted the few stars.
And now the neons thinned, the moon was huge.
The gloomy river lay in a glory, the bridge
In its mists as we rode over it slowly sighed.
We lost the shining tram-lines in the slums
As we kept south; the shining trolley-wires
Glinted through Gorbals; on your helmet a glint hung.
A cat in a crumbling close-mouth, a lighted window
With its shadow-play, a newspaper in the wind—
The night swept them up even as we slowed,
Our wheels jolting over the buckled causeys.
But my net swept up night and cat and road

169

And mine is the shadow-play that window showed
And mine the paper with its cries and creases.
—Shadow-play? What we flashed past was life
As what we flash into is life, and life
Will not stand still until within one flash
Of words or paint or human love it stops
Transfixed, and drops its pain and grime
Into forgetful time.
But I remember: I saw the flash: and then
We met the moonlit Clyde again, swung off
And roared in a straight run for Rutherglen.
The wind whistled by the football ground
And by the waste ground that the seagulls found.
The long wail of a train recalled the city
We had left behind, and mingled with the wind.
Whatever it was that sang in me there
As we neared home, I give it no name here.
But tenements and lives, the wind, our wheels,
The vibrant windshield and your guiding hands
Fell into meaning, whatever meaning it was—
Whatever joy it was—
And my blood quickened in me as I saw
Everything guided, vibrant, where our shadow
Glided along the pavements and the walls.
Perhaps I only saw the thoroughfares,
The river, the dancing of the foundry-flares?
Joy is where long solitude dissolves.
I rode with you towards human needs and cares.

AN ADDITION TO THE FAMILY

A musical poet, collector of basset-horns,
was buttering his toast down in Dunbartonshire
when suddenly from behind the breakfast newspaper
the shining blade stopped scraping
and he cried to his wife, 'Joyce, listen to this!—
"Two basset-hounds for sale, house-trained, keen
     hunters"—

Oh we must have them! What d'you think? . . .' 'But dear,
did you say *hounds*?' 'Yes, yes, hounds, hounds—'
'But Maurice, it's *horns* we want, you must be over
in the livestock column, what would we do
with a basset-hound, you can't play a hound!'
'It's Beverley it says, the kennels are at Beverley—'
'But Maurice—' '—I'll get some petrol, we'll be there by
    lunchtime—'
'But a dog, two dogs, where'll we put them?'
'I've often wondered what these dogs are like—'
'You mean you don't even—' 'Is there no more
    marmalade?'
'—don't know what they look like? And how are we to
    feed them?
Yes, there's the pot dear.' 'This stuff's all peel, isn't it?'
'Well, we're at the end of it. But look, these two great—'
'You used to make marmalade once upon a time.'
'They've got ears down to here, and they're far too—'
'Is that half past eight? I'll get the car out.
See if I left my cheque-book on the—' 'Maurice,
are you mad? What about your horns?' 'What horns,
what are you talking about? Look Joyce dear,
if it's not on the dresser it's in my other jacket.
I believe they're wonderful for rabbits—' . . .

So the musical poet took his car to Beverley
with his wife and his cheque-book, and came back home
with his wife and his cheque-book and two new hostages
to the unexpectedness of fortune.
The creatures scampered through the grass, the children
came out with cries of joy, there seemed to be nothing
dead or dying in all that landscape.
Fortune bless the unexpected cries!
Life gathers to the point of wishing it,
a mocking pearl of many ventures. The house
rolled on its back and kicked its legs in the air.
And later, wondering farmers as they passed would hear
beyond the lighted window in the autumn evening
two handsome yellow-bosomed basset-hounds
howling to a melodious basset-horn.

THE WOMAN

A string of pearls
in the dark window, that wet spring,
sometimes a white hand raised with a cigarette
blurred by rain and buses
anyhow. A lonely
ring.

Nothing she was waiting for
came, unless what took her
in the coldest arms.

It seems to be the pearls
we remember, for what they spoke
of another life than waiting,
and being unknown dying
in a high dark street.

Who she was you'll keep thinking.
The hearse rolled off in thunder,
but showers only lay dust.

FROM FOR BONFIRES

The leaves are gathered, the trees are dying
for a time.
A seagull cries through white smoke in the garden fires
that fill the heavy air.
All day heavy air
is burning, a moody dog
sniffs and circles the swish of the rake.
In streaks of ash, the gardener drifting
ghostly, beats his hands, a cloud
of breath to the red sun.

OBAN GIRL

A girl in a window eating a melon
eating a melon and painting a picture
painting a picture and humming Hey Jude
humming Hey Jude as the light was fading

In the autumn she'll be married

FADO

Fold those waves away
and take the yellow, yellow bay,
roll it up like Saturday.

No use the sleepy sand,
no use my breasts in his brown hand.
I danced on tables in that land.

Grim is my cold sun.
Through my street the long rains run.
Thousands I see, thinking of one.

DONALD MACRAE

THE PTERODACTYL AND POWHATAN'S DAUGHTER

American poets have seen their country
as a brown girl lying serene in the sun,
as Powhatan's daughter with open thighs,
her belly a golden plain of wheat,
her breasts the firm and fecund hills,
each sinuous vein a river, and in each wrist
        the pulse of cataracts.

She has rejected no lover, not the
fanatic English nor the hungry Scot,
the trading Dutchman nor the industrious
continental peasant, used to oppression,
the patient stolen Negro nor the
laborious Asiatic, schooled to diligent,
        ingenious labour.

173

By all her lovers she has been fruitful,
has multiplied all numbers, lying
indolent, calm and almost asleep,
only her lake-eyes watchful, expectant
of new wanderers from further shores
seeking her young immortal body,
      waiting unsated.

She is patient this girl with her black hair tumbled,
with her earth-bedded, receptive body stretched,
relaxed and leisured, at ease in the sun.
In her veins the sun-warm blood is coursing,
swift running through the golden body,
obedient to the steadfast heart's command,
      the unending beat.

Not such is our land. It is a skeleton
crushed by the long weight of years, the bone
hard stone, the skin tight on the sinew,
the flesh wasted by long years of hunger.
It is a stone land, a hard land of bone,
of lean muscle and atrophied membrane
      ridged over ribs.

This is a pterodactyl land,
lean survivor of ice and the frost,
sea and the parching sun, which,
the last of its kind, is now dying
by inches, blinking and bleeding through the
death shroud of mist, the dissolving film
      of steady rain.

We dwell on the stiffening corpse of Scotland,
starved lice on a pauper's body
chill on a marble slab. Should we leave?
Should we follow our father's pattern,
make love to Powhatan's daughter,
westward refurrow the weary sea?
      We had better not.

She too is a myth: we'd be wise to forget
our symbols, turn from the romantic vision,
the loose-thought personified images of countries,
to study and learn to read, painfully,
the facts of these matters aright, then nourish—
if we have heart—some slight sober hope
     of tomorrow.

DERICK THOMSON

CLANN-NIGHEAN AN SGADAIN

An gàire mar chraiteachan salainn
ga fhroiseadh bho 'm bial,
an sàl 's am picil air an teanga,
's na miaran cruinne, goirid a dheanadh giullachd,
no a thogadh leanabh gu socair, cuimir,
seasgair, fallain,
gun mhearachd,
's na sùilean cho domhainn ri fèath.

B'e bun-os-cionn na h-eachdraidh a dh' fhàg iad
'nan tràillean aig ciùrairean cutach,
thall 's a-bhos air Galldachd 's an Sasuinn.
Bu shaillte an duais a thàrr iad
às na mìltean bharaillean ud,
gaoth na mara geur air an craiceann,
is eallach a' bhochdainn 'nan ciste,
is mara b'e an gàire
shaoileadh tu gu robh an teud briste.

Ach bha craiteachan uaille air an cridhe,
ga chumail fallain,
is bheireadh cutag an teanga
slisinn á fanaid nan Gall—
agus bha obair rompa fhathast
nuair gheibheadh iad dhachaidh,
ged nach biodh maoin ac':
air oidhche robach gheamhraidh,
ma bha sud an dàn dhaibh,
dheanadh iad daoine.

THE HERRING GIRLS
from the Gaelic of Derick Thomson
(*English version by Derick Thomson*)

Their laughter like a sprinkling of salt
showered from their lips,
brine and pickle on their tongues,
and the stubby short fingers that could handle fish,
or lift a child gently, neatly, safely, wholesomely,
unerringly,
and the eyes that were as deep as a calm.

The topsy-turvy of history had made them
slaves to short-arsed curers,
here and there in the Lowlands, in England.
Salt the reward they won
from those thousands of barrels,
the sea-wind sharp on their skins,
and the burden of poverty in their kists,
and were it not for their laughter
you might think the harp-string was broken.

But there was a sprinkling of pride in their hearts,
keeping them sound,
and their tongues' gutting-knife
would tear a strip from the Lowlanders' mockery—
and there was work awaiting them
when they got home,
though they had no wealth:
on a wild winter's night,
if that were their lot,
they would make men.

CRUAIDH?

Cuil-lodair, is Briseadh na h-Eaglaise,
is briseadh nan tacannan—
lamhachas-làidir dà thrian de ar comas;
'se seòltachd tha dhìth oirnn.

176

Nuair a theirgeas a' chruaidh air faobhar na speala
caith bhuat a' chlach-lìomhaidh;
chan eil agad ach iarunn bog
mur eil de chruas 'nad innleachd na ni sgathadh.

Is caith bhuat briathran mìne
oir chan fhada bhios briathran agad;
tha Tuatha Dé Danann fo'n talamh.
tha Tìr nan Og anns an Fhraing,
's nuair a ruigeas tu Tìr a' Gheallaidh,
mura bi thu air t' aire,
coinnichidh Sasunnach riut is plìon air,
a dh'innse dhut gun tug Dia, bràthair athar, còir dha às an
    fhearann.

STEEL?
from the Gaelic of Derick Thomson
(English version by Derick Thomson)

Culloden, the Disruption,
and the breaking up of the tack-farms—
two thirds of our power is violence;
it is cunning we need.
When the tempered steel near the edge of the scythe-
    blade is worn,
throw away the whetstone;
you have nothing left but soft iron
unless your intellect has a steel edge that will cut clean.

And throw away soft words,
for soon you will have no words left;
the Tuatha De Danann are underground,
the Land of the Ever-Young is in France,
and when you reach the Promised Land,
unless you are on your toes,
a bland Englishman will meet you,
and say to you that God, his uncle, has given him a title
    to the land.

NUAIR A THILL MI GU T'UAIGH

Nuair a thill mi gu t'uaigh
gu tairiseach, tlàth
cha bu chuimhne leam t'fhiamh.

Bha ceò air mo shùil;
dh'fhalbh seachd is seachd bliadhna
le craiceann nan làmh
a dh'aithnicheadh do chneas;
bhuail na tuinn air mo chlaistneachd;
bha m'iarrtas is m'ùidh
bàthte fo shùgh liath-uaine, fo chlàr
sgith mo bheatha.

Rinn fàileadh nan sìthean tais a' chiad bheàrn
air an sgàile sin 's i seachd-fillte.

Troimh fhilleadh na Sàbaid
chuimhnich mi air do chràbhadh;
troimh fhilleadh Luain
dh'fhairich mi tarraing a' chuain;
troimh fhilleadh Mhàirt
dh' éirich do chruadal an àird;
troimh fhilleadh Chiadain
chunnaic mi thu air chiallaidh;
am filleadh Dhir-daoin
bha do bhanais 's do mhaoin;
fo fhilleadh na h-Aoine
bha 'phìob is na h-òrain fhaoine;
troimh fhilleadh na Sathuirn
dh' aithnich mi nach biodh rath oirnn.

Is bha thu agam—
brèagh, bòidheach, beothant,
milis, mòdhar,
cho diombuain ri flùr,
O shaoghail a bh' ann.

WHEN, TENDER AND MILD
from the Gaelic of Derick Thomson
(English version by Iain Crichton Smith)

When, tender and mild,
I came to your grave,
I could not remember
your frown or your smile.

There were tears in my eyes:
for seven and seven years
had taken the skin
from the hand that once knew
the skin of your flesh.
Waves beat in my ears:
my love and desire
were buried beneath
the grey green ooze
the Minch of my life.

The scent of the flowers
made the first light
in that seven-fold shade.

Through the fold of the Sunday
I knew your devotion;
through the fold of the Monday
the ocean was calling;
through the fold of the Tuesday
your courage arose;
through the fold of the Wednesday
I saw you at fasting;
through the fold of the Thursday
was your gear and your marriage;
through the fold of the Friday
was the piping and singing;
in Saturday's fold
our ill-luck was told.

And I held you, then—
lively and lovely,
sweetly and gently—
O transient flower,
O world that is gone.

STÉIDHICHEAN LÀIDIR

Tha do stéidhichean làidir
anns a' mhuir shàthach sin tha bualadh
's a' suathadh 's a' bragail,
cnap muil air clàr creige.
Do bhallachan air an eagadh
's air a snaidheadh
le locair na mara,
le cruaidh na gaoithe.
Sìtheanan a' fàs orra,
blàth air a' chreig,
is bileagan milis feòir.
Tha do chlachan-oisinn daingeann:
An Rubha Dubh, A' Chàbag, An Gallan;
tha do fhreiceadain-cuain 'nan dùisg.
Nuair dh' fhuilig thu spòltadh nan tonn sin
fuiligidh tu obair mhic-an-duine,
teampall is eaglais is mosque;
thog Nàdur a mhinaret ort,
tha na tuinn ag ùmhlachd aig altair do stallachan,
tha 'n fhaoileag a' frithealadh na h-éifhreann,
tha 'n ùrnuigh air a sleuchdadh ann an cop a' chladaich.

LEWIS
from the Gaelic of Derick Thomson
(English version by Derick Thomson)

Your foundations are strong
in that thrusting sea that thuds
and strokes and cracks,
pebble mass on level rock.
Your walls are notched
and carved
by the plane of the sea,
the chisel of the wind.
Flowers grow on them,
blossom on the rock,
and blades of sweet grass.
Your corner-stones stand firm;
Tolsta Head, Càbag, Gallan Head;
Your sea-watchmen are awake.
Having withstood the mauling of these waves
you can suffer man's work,
temple and church and mosque;
Nature has built on you its minaret,
the waves kneel at the altar of your cliffs,
the seagull celebrates the mass,
the prayer is prostrated in the foam on the shore.

AIR CÙL SHUARDAIL

Gu h-àrd air a' chreig sin,
air cùl Shuardail,
os cionn a' chladaich
far na rinn sinn maorach
air latha samhraidh
bho chionn fhada,
shaoilinn gu faicinn gach nì soilleir;
tha an àile ciùin gun teagamh,
an t-ionad àrd, am muir sàmhach,
gràdh 'na mo chridhe, chan eil an t-eagal
a' cur sgàth orm,
tha Rubha na Circe bàn,

181

tha na reubairean air teicheadh.
Ach cluinnidh mi'n t-òrd aig Thor
fhathast a' cnagadh,
tha eud is murt is cràdh
a' reubadh 's a' sgathadh,
's an gràs a bheireadh sinn á diachainn
air a dhùnadh ann am broinn fiasgain.

BEYOND SWORDALE
from the Gaelic of Derick Thomson
(English version by Derick Thomson)

High on that cliff
beyond Swordale,
above the shore
where we gathered shellfish
on a summer day
long ago,
I would expect to see things clearly;
the air is mild, indeed,
the place high, the sea still,
love in my heart, no fear
casts a shadow on me,
Kirk Point is bare,
the reivers gone.
But I hear Thor's hammer
thudding still,
jealousy, murder, pain
rending and cutting,
and the grace that would save us in the tussle
shut away in the innards of a mussel.

LEODHAS AS T-SAMHRADH

An iarmailt cho soilleir tana
mar gum biodh am brat-sgàile air a reubadh
's an Cruthaidhear 'na shuidhe am fianuis a shluaigh
aig a' bhuntàt 's a sgadan,
gun duine ris an dean E altachadh.

182

'S iongantach gu bheil iarmailt air an t-saoghal
tha cur cho beag a bhacadh air daoine
sealltainn a-steach dha'n an t-sìorruidheachd;
chan eil feum air feallsanachd
far an dean thu chùis le do phrosbaig.

LEWIS IN SUMMER
from the Gaelic of Derick Thomson
(*English version by Derick Thomson*)

The atmosphere clear and transparent
as though the veil had been rent
and the Creator were sitting in full view of His people
eating potatoes and herring,
with no man to whom He can say grace.
Probably there's no other sky in the world
that makes it so easy for people
to look in on eternity;
you don't need philosophy
where you can make do with binoculars.

AN T-EILEAN

Nuair a ràinig sinn an t-eilean
bha feasgar ann
's bha sinn aig fois,
a' ghrian a' dol a laighe
fo chuibhrig cuain
's am bruadar a' tòiseachadh às ùr.

Ach anns a' mhadainn
shad sinn dhinn a' chuibhrig
's anns an t-solus gheal sin
chunnaic sinn loch anns an eilean
is eilean anns an loch,
is chunnaic sinn
gun do theich am bruadar pìos eile bhuainn.

Tha an staran cugallach
chon an dàrna eilein,
tha a' chlach air uideil
tha a' dìon nan dearcag,
tha chraobh chaorainn a' crìonadh,
fàileadh na h-iadhshlait a' faileachdainn oirnn a nis.

THE ISLAND
from the Gaelic of Derick Thomson
(*English version by Derick Thomson*)

When we reached the island
it was evening
and we were at peace,
the sun lying down
under the sea's quilt
and the dream beginning anew.

But in the morning
we tossed the cover aside
and in that white light
saw a loch in the island,
and an island in the loch,
and we recognized
that the dream had moved away from us again.

The stepping-stones are chancy
to the second island,
the stone totters
that guards the berries,
the rowan withers,
we have lost now the scent of the honeysuckle.

THE OLD WOMEN

Go sad or sweet or riotous with beer
Past the old women gossiping by the hour,
They'll fix on you from every close and pier
An acid look to make your veins run sour.

'No help,' they say, 'his grandfather that's dead
Was troubled with the same dry-throated curse,
And many a night he made the ditch his bed.
This blood comes welling from the same cracked source.'

On every kind of merriment they frown.
But I have known a gray-eyed sober boy
Sail to the lobsters in a storm, and drown.
Over his body dripping on the stones
Those same old hags would weave into their moans
An undersong of terrible holy joy.

THE LODGING

The stones of the desert town
Flush; and, a star-filled wave,
Night steeples down.

From a pub door here and there
A random ribald song
Leaks on the air.

The Roman in a strange land
Broods, wearily leaning
His lance in the sand.

The innkeeper over the fire
Counting his haul, hears not
The cry from the byre;

185

But rummaging in the till
Grumbles at the drunken shepherds
Dancing on the hill;

And wonders, pale and grudging,
If the queer pair below
Will pay their lodging.

TROUT FISHER

Semphill, his hat stuck full of hooks
    Sits drinking ale
        Among the English fishing visitors,
    Probes in detail
            Their faults in casting, reeling, selection of flies.
'Never,' he urges, 'do what it says in the books.'
            Then they, obscurely wise,
        Abandon by the loch their dripping oars
And hang their throttled tarnish on the scale.

'Forgive me, every speckled trout,'
    Says Semphill then,
        'And every swan and eider on these waters.
    Certain strange men,
            Taking advantage of my poverty
Have wheedled all my subtle loch-craft out
            So that their butchery
        Seem fine technique in the ear of wives and daughters
And I betray the loch for a white coin.'

WEDDING

With a great working of elbows
The fiddlers ranted
        —Joy to Ingrid and Magnus!

With much boasting and burning
The whisky circled
        —Wealth to Ingrid and Magnus!

186

With deep clearings of the throat
The minister intoned
    —Thirdly, Ingrid and Magnus. . . .

Ingrid and Magnus stared together
When midnight struck
At a white unbroken bed.

HAMNAVOE MARKET

They drove to the market with ringing pockets.
    Folster found a girl
Who put wounds on his face and throat,
Small diagonal wounds like red doves.
    Johnstone stood beside the barrel.
All day he stood there.
He woke in a ditch, his mouth full of ashes.
    Grieve bought a balloon and a goldfish.
He swung through the air.
He fired shotguns, rolled pennies, ate sweet fog from a stick.
    Heddle was at the Market also.
I know nothing of his activities.
He is and always was a quiet man.
    Garson fought three rounds with a Negro boxer
And received thirty shillings,
Much applause, and an eye loaded with thunder.
    Where did they find Flett?
They found him in a brazen ring
Of blood and fire, a new Salvationist.
    A gipsy saw in the hand of Halcro
Great strolling herds, harvests, a proud woman.
He wintered in the poorhouse.

They drove home from the Market, under the stars,
Except for Johnstone
Who lay in a ditch, his mouth full of dying fires.

OLD FISHERMAN WITH GUITAR

A formal exercise for withered fingers.
  The head is bent,
    The eyes half closed, the tune
Lingers
    And beats, a gentle wing the west had thrown
    Against his breakwater wall with salt savage lament.

So fierce and sweet the song on the plucked string,
  Know now for truth
    These hands have cut from the net
The strong
    Crab-eaten corpse of Jock washed from a boat
  One old winter, and gathered the mouth of Thora to
      his mouth.

THE POET

Therefore he no more troubled the pool of silence
But put on mask and cloak,
Strung a guitar
And moved among the folk.
Dancing they cried,
'Ah, how our sober islands
Are gay again, since this blind lyrical tramp
Invaded the Fair!'

Under the last dead lamp
When all the dancers and masks had gone inside
His cold stare
Returned to its true task, interrogation of silence.

HADDOCK FISHERMEN

Midnight. The wind yawing nor-east.
A low blunt moon.
Unquiet beside quiet wives we rest.

A spit of rain and a gull
In the open door.
The lit fire. A quick mouthful of ale.

We push the *Merle* at a sea of cold flame.
The oars drip honey.
Hook by hook uncoils under The Kame.

Our line breaks the trek of sudden thousands.
Twelve nobbled jaws,
Gray cowls, gape in our hands.

Twelve cold mouths scream without sound.
The sea is empty again.
Like tinkers the bright ones endlessly shift their ground.

We probe emptiness all the afternoon,
Then pause and fill our teeth
With dependable food, beef and barley scone.

Sunset drags its butcher blade
From the day's throat.
We turn through an ebb salt and sticky as blood.

More stars than fish. Women, cats, a gull
Mewl at the rock.
The valley divides the meagre miracle.

UNLUCKY BOAT

That boat has killed three people. Building her
Sib drove a nail through his thumb, and died in his croft
Bunged to the eyes with rust and penicillin.
One evening when the Flow was a bar of silver
Under the moon, and Mansie and Tom with wands
Were putting a spell on cuithes, she dipped a bow
And ushered Mansie, his pipe still in his teeth,
To meet the cold green angels. They hauled her up
Among the rocks, right in the path of Angus,

Whose neck, rigid with pints from the Dounby market,
Snapped like a barley stalk . . . There she lies,
A leprous unlucky bitch, in the quarry of Moan.

Tinkers, going past, make the sign of the cross.

FIDDLER'S SONG

The storm is over, lady.
The sea makes no more sound.
What do you wait for, lady?
His yellow hair is drowned.

The waves go quiet, lady,
Like sheep into the fold.
What do you wait for, lady?
His kissing mouth is cold.

IAN HAMILTON FINLAY

BLACK TOMINTOUL

To Scotland came the tall American
And went to stay on a little farm
Oh it was a Scotch farm set in the wild
A wee Scotch burn and a stony field

She came to a corner, it was raining
And the little trees were all leaning in
This was Scotland the way she had thought of it
Care, not gravity, makes them lean
The rain falling Scotchly, Scotchly
And the hills that did not soar up but in

But most she looked at the bull so wild
She looked at the bull with the eyes of a child
Never in New York did she see such a bull
As this great Scotch one, Tomintoul
She called him secretly, the great Scotch bull

He was black all over, even for a bull
And oh he had such a lovely hide
She saw him follow one cow aside
Tell me, please, is that cow his bride?
No, they are all his lawful br-r-ride
There were twenty-four cows on the Scotch hillside

It was almost too much for the tall American girl
She watched him stand on his opposite hill
Black Tomintoul, and he always bellowed
But afterwards something in her was mellowed.

BEDTIME

So put your nightdress on
It is so white and long
And your sweet night-face
Put it on also please
It is the candle-flame
It is the flame above
Whose sweet shy shame
My love, I love, I love.

ALASTAIR MACKIE

MONGOL QUINE

Elbucks on the herbour waa
the mongol quine
collogues
wi hersel.

Her blonde baa-heid wags
frae side to side.
Noo she's a clock-hand
noo a croon.

Wha said grace and grouwin
tae this mistak?
A ban was on her
frae furder back.

Nievie nievie nack nack
whit hand'll ye tak tak?
She got the wrang hand
and didna pan oot.

She's got pig's een,
a bannock face,
and hurdies that rowed
like twa muckle bools.

She wints for naething. Yet
she's singin till the distance.
Ayont the hert-brak her een
are set for ever on an unkent airt.

IN ABSENTIA

'We've no heard frae God this while,'
said ane o the angels.
It was at a synod
o the metaphors.

Cam a wind;
it was aabody speirin
'Wha?'
intill themsels.

It was heard by the sauls
o Baudelaire and Pascal.
They fell thro the muckle hole
opened by the question.

I the boddom Jesus sweatit
'Consummatum est.'

And Nietzsche
hou he laucht and laucht.

The maist o fowk bein neither
philosophers or theologians
kept gaun tae the kirk.
Whiles, like.

Syne God said: 'Noo I'm awa,
mak a kirk or a mill o't.'

And God gaed tae the back o beyond
i the midst o aathing.

ALASTAIR REID

GHOSTS' STORIES

That bull-necked blotch-faced farmer from Drumlore
would never dream (or so we heard him boast
to neighbours at the lamb sales in Kirkcudbright)
of paying the least attention to a ghost.

Were we to blame for teaching him a lesson?
We whored his daughter, spaded all his ewes,
brought a blight on his barley, drew the sea
rampaging over his sod . . .

If we had any doubt that he deserved it,
that went when we heard him stamp his ruined acres
and blame it all on God.

When we went on and frightened Miss McQueen
for keeping children in on Halloween,
and wailed all night in the schoolhouse, she, poor woman,
sent for the Fire Brigade.
And so we made
fire lick from her hair, till they put her out.

The children knew what it was all about.

193

THE FIGURES ON THE FRIEZE

Darkness wears off, and, dawning into light,
they find themselves unmagically together.
He sees the stains of morning in her face.
She shivers, distant in his bitter weather.

Diminishing of legend sets him brooding.
Great goddess-figures conjured from his book
blur what he sees with bafflement of wishing.
Sulky, she feels his fierce, accusing look.

Familiar as her own, his body's landscape
seems harsh and dull to her habitual eyes.
Mystery leaves, and, mercilessly flying,
the blind fiends come, emboldened by her cries.

Avoiding simple reach of hand for hand
(which would surrender pride) by noon they stand
withdrawn from touch, reproachfully alone,
small in each other's eyes, tall in their own.

Wild with their misery, they entangle now
in baffling agonies of why and how.
Afternoon glimmers, and they wound anew,
flesh, nerve, bone, gristle in each other's view.

'What have you done to me?' From each proud heart,
new phantoms walk in the deceiving air.
As the light fails, each is consumed apart,
he by his ogre vision, she by her fire.

When night falls, out of a despair of daylight,
they strike the lying attitudes of love,
and through the perturbation of their bodies,
each feels the amazing, murderous legends move.

PROPINQUITY

is the province of cats. Living by accident,
lapping the food at hand, or sleeking down
in an adjacent lap when sleep occurs to them,
never aspiring to consistency
in homes or partners, unaware of property,
cats take their chances, love by need and nearness
as long as the need lasts, as long as the nearness
is near enough. The code of cats is simply
to take what comes. And those poor souls who claim
to own a cat, who long to recognize
in bland and narrowing eyes a look like love,
are bound to suffer should they expect
cats to come purring punctually home.
Home is only where the food and the fire are,
but might be anywhere. Cats fall on their feet,
nurse their own wounds, attend to their own laundry,
and purr at appropriate times. O folly, folly
to love a cat, and yet
we dress with love the distance that they keep,
the hair-raising way they have, and easily blame
all the abandoned litters and torn ears
on some marauding tiger. Well, no matter;
cats do not care.
    Yet part of us is cat. Confess—
love turns on accident, and needs
nearness; and the various selves we have
all come from our cat-wanderings, our chance
crossings. Imagination prowls at night,
cat-like among odd possibilities.
Only our dog-sense brings us faithfully homeward,
makes meaning out of accident, keeps faith,
and, cat-and-dog, the arguments go at it.
But every night, outside, cat-voices call
us out to take a chance, to leave
the safety of our baskets, and to let
what happens, happen. 'Live, live!' they catcall.
'Each moment is your next! Propinquity,
propinquity is all!'

TO A CHILD AT THE PIANO

Play the tune again; not watching
with more regard for the movement at the source of it,
and less attention to time. Time falls
curiously in the course of it.

Play the tune again; not watching
your fingering, but forgetting, letting flow
the sound till it surrounds you. Do not count
or even think. Let go.

Play the tune again; but try to be
nobody, nothing, as though the pace
of the sound were your heart beating, as though
the music were your face.

Play the tune again. It should be easier
to think less every time of the notes, of the measure.
It is all an arrangement of silence. Be silent, and then
play it for your pleasure.

Play the tune again; and this time, when it ends,
do not ask me what I think. Feel what is happening
strangely in the room as the sound glooms over
you, me, everything.

Now,
play the tune again.

TREND SPOTTER

There's a magpie keeps jolting me awake at dawn
with peremptory beak-taps on my window glass.

I'm flattered by his attention, but suspect
I'm one of many he has under observation.

Not knowing his intention bothers me. What
if he's doing field-work on the human factor?

Can my case be taken as representative
of an entire generation, or am I tagged

forever, 'Lesser Stubbled Attic Rooster',
in some definitive quill-flourishing thesis?

The nicest people study social sciences
but a magpie sociologist is too much!

He'll gobble fresh-hatched theories, and pick up
anything that takes his fancy for a survey.

His nest stuffed with smatterings of motley jargon;
pauperbeak psychology and ad-man droppings.

Food and feathers and the Golden Bough were all
he believed in before this preoccupation.

But perhaps it's all delusion, and it's his own
image he's knocking, quite unaware of mine.

HOMELY ACCOMMODATION, SUIT GENT

In that repository of auction pots and post-Ark
furniture, stepping over the creaking board
you always sprang another, setting Mrs Hagglebroth

197

ready to intercept you with her pleated smile
and plucked eyebrows up, while conducting her
wallpaper centenary festival with a stick of feathers.

In that saddlesoap atmosphere, there was no music
after Mozart, and no smoking in the dining-room.
Sunlight was discouraged: it fades the draperies.
Sunday papers she detested, like all dirt. Even
the bought earth was sterilized before the bulbs,
one to a pot, were planted; God rest their souls.

But the remarkable strain of slaughterhouse fly
that bloated its dipstick in her best insecticide
always escaped her notice, though she stiffened
at irregular movements of bedsprings, and blushed
when the cistern gargled openly. Somehow her gentlemen
kept moving on, though she prayed for them all.

It was as if, when the seed stirred in them, they
thought of her with rubber gloves on, oiling her shears,
and fled, a week overpaid. Behind her back, when
she went to church, talk about wart-hogs in war-togs,
they called her Brothelhag, bartering sniggers,
and the sweat chilled on them in case she knew.

One lay awake at night sheeted in terror, when
the Hagglebroth bloomers billowing from the line
rose in binocular glory and loomed at his window
like a zeppelin. He left. They all left. Even
the glutted fly. Finally Mrs Hagglebroth herself
left, in a brand-new box sealed against sunlight.

So we have here the Hagglebroth effects. The souls
of miscellaneous gentlemen, welded to wicker chairs.
The fears of young men and the dread of old, potted
in antique brass. Several conscience racks, disguised
as beds. Connoisseur stuff, all of it. So come now,
ladies, you have your catalogues. . . . What am I bid?

LUSS VILLAGE

Such walls, like honey, and the old are happy
in morphean air like gold-fish in a bowl.
Ripe roses trail their margins down a sleepy
mediaeval treatise on the slumbering soul.

And even the water, fabulously silent,
has no salt tales to tell us, nor makes jokes
about the yokel mountains, huge and patient,
that will not court her but read shadowy books.

A world so long departed! In the courtyard
the tilted tombs still gossip, and the leaves
of stony testaments are read by Richard,
Jean and Carol, pert among the sheaves

of unscythed meadows, while the noon day hums
with bees and water and the ghosts of psalms.

OLD WOMAN

And she, being old, fed from a mashed plate
as an old mare might droop across a fence
to the dull pastures of its ignorance.
Her husband held her upright while he prayed

to God who is all-forgiving to send down
some angel somewhere who might land perhaps
in his foreign wings among the gradual crops.
She munched, half dead, blindly searching the spoon.

Outside, the grass was raging. There I sat
imprisoned in my pity and my shame
that men and women having suffered time
should sit in such a place, in such a state

and wished to be away, yes, to be far away
with athletes, heroes, Greeks or Roman men
who pushed their bitter spears into a vein
and would not spend an hour with such decay.

'Pray God,' he said, 'we ask you, God,' he said.
The bowed back was quiet. I saw the teeth
tighten their grip around a delicate death.
And nothing moved within the knotted head

but only a few poor veins as one might see
vague wishless seaweed floating on a tide
of all the salty waters where had died
too many waves to mark two more or three.

TWO GIRLS SINGING

It neither was the words nor yet the tune.
Any tune would have done and any words.
Any listener or no listener at all.

As nightingales in rocks or a child crooning
in its own world of strange awakening
or larks for no reason but themselves.

So on the bus through late November running
by yellow lights tormented, darkness falling,
the two girls sang for miles and miles together

and it wasn't the words or tune. It was the singing.
It was the human sweetness in that yellow,
the unpredicted voices of our kind.

THE WITCHES

Coveys of black witches gather
at corners, closes.
Their thin red noses
are in among the mash of scandal.

Poking red fires with
intense breath, hot as the imagined
rape riding the hot mind.
The real one was more moral

and more admirable because animal.
In an empty air they convene
their red, sad, envious, beaks. The clean
winter rubs them raw

in a terrible void, hissing
with tongues of winter fire.
Pity them, pity them. Dare
to ring them with your love.

THE CEMETERY NEAR BURNS' COTTAGE

Tombs of the Covenanters nod together
grey heads and obstinate. They saw them come
the silver horsemen meditating murder
but stood there quietly to the beating drum
of God and psalm, the heart's immaculate order.

So now I see them as the churchyard turns
red in the evening light. They did not know
that moral milk turns sour, and something churns
inside the stony cask. This churchyard now
flickers with light, untameably with Burns,

the secret enemy within the stone,
the hand which even here stings its hot whip
in glittering rays from socketed bone to bone.
In such fixed Eden did his changing shape
unlock their teeth from what they'd bravely won.

201

THE TEMPTATION

Imagine, say, a mediaeval window
quietly painting grass from its studied green.
Imagine a monk or two soberly walking,
both gown and soul immaculately clean.
Also, behind them, a fine passage of birds
like a taste of Latin, a clear sip of Greek.
Imagine them walking like this, too quiet to speak.

And say you imagine it well, the hum of learning,
that queenless hive, a manuscript inlaid
with the whipped body's colours. (Say a sun
had gaily pierced a black devilish cloud.)
Imagine also a fine hush of prayer,
a library where God might be caught
dining perhaps on a Vergilian thought.

You might be tempted, yes, you might be tempted
till you remembered the draughts of cold rooms,
a sort of love gone wrong, a false devotion,
snarled horses smoking past in windy glooms,
and you might say yes: Yes, it was very well,
yes, there was something, but suppose a man
laughed at and burnt to a sacked autumn grain.

And also remember well the stake, the jeering
in a religious drizzle, while the calm
angels surrounded God at shining tables.
Directions glittered on a soldier's helm.
The page was warm and green in monkish hands
but there, outside, a man was bent in two
to teach him that his arrows must fly true.

OLD WOMAN

Your thorned back
heavily under the creel
you steadily stamped the rising daffodil.

Your set mouth
forgives no one, not even God's justice
perpetually drowning law with grace.

Your cold eyes
watched your drunken husband come
unsteadily from Sodom home.

Your grained hands
dandled full and sinful cradles.
You built for your children stone walls.

Your yellow hair
burned slowly in a scarf of grey
wildly falling like the mountain spray.

Finally you're alone
among the unforgiving brass,
the slow silences, the sinful glass.

Who never learned,
not even ageing, to forgive
our poor journey and our common grave

while the free daffodils
wave in the valleys and on the hills
the deer look down with their instinctive skills,

and the huge sea
in which your brothers drowned sings slow
over the headland and the peevish crow.

HIGHLAND PORTRAIT

Castles draw in their horns. The stones are streaming
with fine Highland rain. A woman's struggling
against the sour wet wind in a black skirt.
Mist on the mountains. Waterfalls are pouring
their tons of water with a hollow roaring.
The phantom chieftans pass the heavy port.

Fences straggle westwards. Absurd cattle
lift their shaggy heads through humming water.
A duck dives coolly into stylish seas.
Hotels are sleeping in their winter colours.
The oilskinned sailors wear their gleaming yellows.
Glencoes are wailing in the hollow trees.

Country of céilidhs and the delicate manners,
obstinate dowagers of emerald honours,
the rain has worn your metaphors away.
Only poor rays of similes are shining
from brooches and from buckles. The complaining
barren rocks and ravens fill the day.

Nothing to say except a world has ended.
The waters of Polldubh, direct and splendid,
will hump unsteady men to a boiling death.
Yet from the shaking bridge of fascination
we see in these the antiseptic passion
whose surgeon's reason is a kind of birth.

YOUNG GIRL

Nothing more impermanent, it appears,
in your bare nylons twittering. The harsh

waves will not overwhelm you as you rock
on tottering heels towards the yellow clock

high on the windy pier. You toughly peck
at your oiled bag of chips, as seagulls break

herring heads like egg-shells, with bulb eyes.
I watch you in your sheer indomitableness

click the late street past yellow cafe light,
an H.M.S. that's joining the grey fleet.

204

A LETTER

Tonight I'll meet you: yes, tonight. I know
There are, perhaps, a thousand miles—but not
Tonight. Tonight I go inside. I take
All the walls down, the bric-à-brac, the trash,
The tawdry pungent dust these months have gathered
Into a heap about me. I must prepare
And somehow move away from the slow world,
The circling menace with its throat and teeth
Attempting definition; and brush off
Those thoughts that, clinging like thin fallen hairs,
Make me unclean; for I must go tonight
And, secret from my shadow, go alone
Back to the hour when you yourself became
So much my own that even my own eyes
Seemed strange compared to you who were a new
Complete pervasive organ of all sense
Through which I saw and heard and more than touched
The very dignity of experience.

TREE

Tree. Tree. Do you want to become a man?
A woman then? A wren in your branches?
You, tree, who stand stiller than I can,
    Do you want to move?
To flicker away from me, safely and swiftly away,
    Then slacken up to say:
You are mine; I am yours? O tree, do you want to love?

You stand, tree, in the thick grass,
Upright, unquenchably still. A man passes.
But you, tree, stand still, and still as stained glass
    Gather the light
In a green bouquet, gather it up and spill
    Shadows about you until
With a dark splash like a beacon I wade in your night.

Then I look up, tree, from at your feet:
Sunlight splits into a shrapnel pattern;
Leaves become black and the black leaves meet
        In layers on air,
Tenderly frisking, yet stubborn under the wind,
    And stubbornly in my mind
Remaining delicate though your black boughs glare.

    I think, thus looking, that perhaps some gnomes
    In buried places where they are homely
    Must busily, when the sky becomes
        Top-heavy with light,
Lift you up chirruping to its zenith and
    Brush the whole sky with green land
Till its looks like earth, earth photographed in flight.

    Or that the clouds, which frolic and glare,
    And sly as a weasel, furry, unfearing,
    Have let you down from their pleasant nowhere
        And bundled you high.
Tree. Tree. Symmetrical bonfire, igneous green,
    What did earth's heavens mean
When they let you fall then filled you with the sky?

    You do not care. You'll not be caring
    Whether or no it means that the queer
    Energy through you is disappearing
        With nothing more given,
That empty gravities from an empty earth
    Are throwing themselves through your girth
Until they can connect with empty heaven.

    Or, if you do, how can I tell,
    From the greedy cell where I guard myself
    And count the worlds of me that kill
        Neighbours with nearness,
How can I hope to understand you, tree,
    You, the arch-stranger to me
Who cannot reach my own articulate clearness?

206

I stand beneath you and you build halls
Like filigreed cobwebs out of valleys
Or over my head where the slant light falls
    You spill your sheaves
Of garnered shade about me, changing its
    Brilliance to brilliance that splits
Leathery, lush, an involved aether of leaves.

I, the supreme animal, I man,
Dream up shapelier than the land
That nourishes you, or the sun can.
    I who create
A mythology out of your driest twig, who can make
    Your thickest timbers break,
I ask you to enter into my own estate.

Crouch your great body into this
Sweating sensitive skin, and listen:
These eyes watch, these lips kiss,
    This heart breaks:
But you, for all your gusty lunges, can't
    Even begin to want
The love that feeds you or the truth that takes.

You could have motion to teach you how
Nothing ever departs slowly:
You could have language itself to show
    Why hope must fail:
And finally, climactic in your mind,
    You'd know that you were blind
And other knowledge is impossible.

For I, as I stand sweetly here,
Look up at you and see you clearly
As one more thing I can't come near
    From above or below,
Discover you will never want to be
    Anything other than tree
And understand the thing I do not know.

207

Yes. I am man. I cannot wish
Anything other than my own foolish
Need to change shape and so to brush
    The air like you
And shoot long roots beneath me into earth.
    I deny myself rebirth
By wishing to be born again anew.

This play between us, you and me,
Proceeds by laws that bind us freely,
Me into man, you into tree,
    Together today.
There is a sufficient mystery here with you.
    Draw apart. We are two.
All this, all is sufficient. I go on my way.

I move away downhill over lawns
Where the evening buttercup looks like dawning
Into a warm reply to the songs
    I suffer by.
You shake your birds' nests in the twilit wind.
    You do not follow my kind.
You stand, arms open to receive the sky.

PETERHEAD IN MAY

Small lights pirouette
Among these brisk little boats.
A beam, cool as a butler,
Steps from the lighthouse.

Wheelroom windows are dark.
Reflections of light quickly
Skip over them tipsily like
A girl in silk.

One knows there is new paint
And somehow an intense
Suggestion of ornament
Comes into mind.

Imagine elephants here.
They'd settle, clumsily sure
Of themselves and of us and of four
Square meals and of water.

Then you will have it. This
Though a grey and quiet place
Finds nothing much amiss.
It keeps its stillness.

There is no wind. A thin
Mist fumbles above it and,
Doing its best to be gone,
Obscures the position.

HOME FROM SEA

The longest days are those spent at sea.
Waves dip heavily, trundling under our gunwale
An imagination or promise of the ocean as abyss.
The longest days are those we can hardly remember.
Dead waters retire. The smoke lingers unshaven
Or lounges from cabins into a corridor where
It collides helplessly with the stink of coffee.

There is no steadiness anywhere except in the arrival
Of another wave or another morning. The same
Unsteadiness, waves morning by morning,
Jolts without jest our neurotic banter.

Slowly around us the air circulates like
A paper that everyone has already re-read
And will re-read later. Ghostly
The engines clamber through the floor.

Cards collect grease from many fingers. Dust
Rubs along the ward-room to the galley.
The great sea collapses harmlessly outside
An unopening door.

209

Slipshod and sleepy, we calculate who we are,

We sit beside the clock that thuds so softly
Around its circles and dictates our duties.
Its monosyllables never threaten us.
We know we're safe; since, though the ocean flexes
Its watery muscles with a vast display,
There is inside those ships which sail the farthest
A shabby but invulnerable place that hedges
Stability with repetitive concision.

The clock, in monosyllables, repeats,
Time out of mind and out of time with ours,
A mile, a mile, another mile, until
One day it stops, neglected, unwound,
The current turned off: this is our destination.

TOM BUCHAN

THE WEEK-END NATURALIST

My humanoid friend, myself, a limited animal
in love with the planet
escaping across the dumb topographies of Assynt
with maps and a compass
taking incorrect fixes on anonymous Bens
staring into bog-pools

entertaining myself with half-formulated notions
of a non-utilitarian character
and applying my ragbag of ecological data
to flowers which I recognize
absentmindedly as if they were old friends
whose names I've forgotten

timidly leaping backwards at the green skeleton
of a ewe
scared out of my wits by an equally terrified stag
and always very much conscious
of my wet socks, my deaf ear, balding pate
and over-filled gut

but retaining even here persistent after-images
of my bank-balance
the impersonal malevolence of ill-paid officials
the pretensions
of well-paid academics, the dishonesties of shopkeepers
car-salesmen and politicians

until my vague fountain of speculative ideas
coalesces into irritability
and these innocent towers of darkening gneiss
stand over me
like tax inspectors as I trip on a delinquent peat
and fall on my face.

SCOTLAND THE WEE

Scotland the wee, crèche of the soul,
of thee I sing

land of the millionaire draper, whisky vomit
and the Hillman Imp

staked out with church halls, gaelic sangs
and the pan loaf

eventide home for teachers and christians,
nirvana of the keelie imagination

Stenhousemuir, Glenrothes, Auchterarder, Renton
—one way street to the coup of the mind.

THE EVERLASTING ASTRONAUTS

These dead astronauts cannot decay—
they bounce on the quilted walls of their tin grave
and very gently collide with polythene balloons
full of used mouthwash, excrements and foodscraps.

They were chosen not for their imagination
but for their compatibility with machines—
glancing out at the vast America of the universe
they cried, 'Gee boys, it's great up here!'

Now, tumbling and yawing, their playpen hurries
into the continuum and at last they are real explorers
voyaging endlessly among unrecorded splendours
with Columbus, Peary, Magellan and Drake.

ANNE B. MURRAY

FROST ROUND THE HOUSE

There is no sound under the frost.
Tonight it is as though the walls are frozen too
So intense is this silence, this stillness.
Nothing moves at all
And I wonder,
What sounds usually fill the evenings
When winter and darkness bend houses to the earth?
Usually there is sound or I wouldn't notice the lack.
There is no creak of a robbing wind unwary on rafters
No sound of a window's struggle.
There is no murmur from outside from the deeps of the
    tumbled burn
No muted mutter of trees and waves.
There is no sound.
All round the house the night sits hunched as an owl
Feathered and still
But more still than the night,
Inside the house
Is the curious listening of the air—
Yet
There is no sound to hear.

MY FAITHER

Staunin noo aside his braw bress-haunled coffin
I mind him fine aside the black shinin range
In his grey strippit trousers, galluses and nae collar
For the flannel shirt. My faither.

I ken him fine thae twenty and mair years ago
Wi his great bauchles and flet auld kep;
And in his pooch the spottit reid neepkin
For usin wi snuff. My faither.

And ben in the lobby abune the braw shoon and spats,
Aside the silk waistcoat and claw-haimmer jaicket
Wi its muckle oxter pooch, hung the lum hat.
They caa'd him Jock the Lum. My faither.

And noo staunin wi thae braw shinin haunles
See him and me baith laid oot in the best
Black suitin wi proper white all weel chosen.
And dinna ken him. *My faither.*

staunin—standing   bress-haunled—brass-handled   galluses—braces
bauchles—old shoes   flet auld kep—flat old cap   pooch—pocket
muckle oxter—big shoulder   lum hat—silk hat   baith—both   dinna
ken—don't know

TODD

My father's white uncle became
Arthritic and testamental in
Lyrical stages. He held cardinal sin
Was misuse of horses, then any game

Won on the sabbath. A Clydesdale
To him was not bells and sugar or declension
From paddock, but primal extension
Of rock and soil. Thundered nail

Turned to sacred bolt. And each night
In the stable he would slaver and slave
At cracked hooves, or else save
Bowls of porridge for just the right

Beast. I remember I lied
To him once, about oats: then I felt
The brand of his loving tongue, the belt
Of his own horsey breath. But he died,

When the mechanised tractor came to pass.
Now I think of him neighing to some saint
In a simple heaven or, beyond complaint,
Leaning across a fence and munching grass.

THE CLEARING

Woodsmoke, sheer grapebloom, smears
The trunks of trees, tricks larches
Lilac, and as deftly clears.
Startlingly, among patches

Of sunlight, come glints
Of steel: the woodmen are at it
Early. Red-jerkined, gigantic
In quirk lighting, they flit

Under branches, make markings
Or, smirched, become blurs
Of themselves. Somewhere a dog barks.
Hand-saws spark, and sputter.

Breaking cover, a brood
Of partridges wheedles
Through charlock. Lopped wood,
Crippling down, sends needles

Showering. Blades whirr; logs are
Rolled and chained. Crushed
Brushwood leaks. Air
Is spiced with resin and sawdust.

Then they are gone, to the sound
Of singing. Where pathways join,
Fires flicker. And the ground
Is littered with huge and copper coins.

VISITING HOUR

In the pond of our new garden
were five orange stains, under
inches of ice. Weeks since anyone
had been there. Already by far
the most severe winter for years.
You broke the ice with a hammer.
I watched the goldfish appear,
blunt-nosed and delicately clear.

Since then so much has taken place
to distance us from what we were.
That it should come to this.
Unable to hide the horror
in my eyes, I stand helpless
by your bedside and can do no more
than wish it were simply a matter
of smashing the ice and giving you air.

ROBIN FULTON

FORECAST FOR A QUIET NIGHT

A secret cone will drop in Rothiemurcus,
causing not the slightest local disturbance.

A quiet wind will stroke Loch Araich-linn,
an indiscretion no one can possibly notice.

215

By dawn imperceptible frosty wrinkles
will have puckered the edges of countless backwaters.

By dawn too a generation of mice
will have been snipped by a night-shift of owls
working separately and almost in silence.

And the mild local disturbance behind the eyes
of the invalid
will have been noted only by the next of kin.

FROM SEVEN SONGS FOR A COOL MAN

Don't touch the trees—their soft bark will suck your
    fingers dry.
Don't touch the water—it will open once for you, then
    you'll be gone.

Don't touch the flower, don't touch the bird, don't touch
    the cat,
there is nothing left to touch but each other and our
    skins are cracked leather.

What can you do in a dismal garden hung with veils of
    grey mist?
Hold yourself tight . . . but the mist seeps in, you breathe
    it out and in.

You offer me a stone that's small and hard and say 'Let's
    pretend it's an apple.'
You pretend to be a tree and drop the stone/apple into
    my waiting hand.

I take it because giving and taking small things is all there
    is left to do.
I take it because I want forbidden fruit—only pretending
    will have to do.

216

Don't look, but the garden is drying out: if we stand here
    much longer
Trees will spray like roman candles, real apples explode, our
    bodies curl to a cinder.

THE LAST BOAT OF THE SEASON

1

Somewhere outside, sky and sea
are one indistinguishable black.

Motto for the day has been: *will visitors
please leave, the boat is ready to sail.*

Town after town, horizon after horizon,
on every platform and quay the waving people
have shrunk and vanished most quickly of all . . .

We must be stars in an expanding galaxy
pulled further and further apart from one another.

The vodka in my glass sways gently, a small
but clear measure of what's happening beneath.
I drink it up. The empty glass tells nothing.

2

The night train echoes in the pinewoods.
At every crossing the warning-bell clangs.

My dreams too show a doppler effect,
distorting faces and words as they approach,
as they leave: total clarity only
for a microsecond.

Tomorrow, waiting: the last boat of the season.
Tonight, the train's already past your horizon,
known about but unseen, like an atom.
We can trust our eyes only at arm's length.

I look at my watch every five minutes:
a green luminous smudge in the dark, the earth
seen by an astronaut having a bad night.
I take it off and smother it under my pillow.

The ghosts say 'We are eternal', and depart.
Mahogany Hall Stomp plays them out.

The richly dying trees are dying invisibly.
My own thoughts tinge in the acid soil . . .
I'm in the dark between two landscapes.

The days and the music can always be played again,
fresh candles lit.
We know about the departure of eternal things.

What's left? Your hand on my watch to hide the time.

STEPHEN MULRINE

WOMAN'S COMPLAINT

If, husband, I should say,
   'A young man looked at me today,
   took pleasure in my lower lip,
   knelt down in fabled sand to clip
   me naked in his arms,' would it surprise
you? Yet he did, and in his eyes
I might have played oblivious, desired
his delta fingers to enrich my tired
hair, his drying mouth to crush
my matronly objections. But the blush
I cost him turning snapped the spell,
and in its spread I watched him tell
my years. And though we shared,
husband, nothing else, that moment stared
us down, to years, to unkept rage.
And if I were to say, husband, 'Age
   does not creep up on a woman; decay
   is an instant discerned in the play

218

    of young hunger and young self-respect
    over faded erotica,' would it affect
you? Would you write sonnets, fight duels, deny that I'm
      old?
Or does all this leave you, as me, mortally cold?

THE COMING OF THE WEE MALKIES

Whit'll ye dae when the wee Malkies come,
if they dreep doon affy the wash-hoose dyke
an' pit the hems oan the sterrheid light,
an' play wee headies oan the clean close-wa',
an' blooter yir windae in wi' the ba',
missis, whit'll ye dae?

Whit'll ye dae when the wee Malkies come,
if they chap yir door an' choke the drain,
an' caw the feet frae yir sapsy wean,

an' tummle thur wulkies through yir sheets,
an' tim thur ashes oot in the street,
missis, whit'll ye dae?

Whit'll ye dae when the wee Malkies come,
if they chuck thur screwtaps doo the pan,
an' stick the heid oan the sanit'ry man;
when ye hear thum come shauchlin' doon yir loaby,
chantin', 'Wee Malkies! The gemme's . . . a bogey!'
haw, missis, whit'll ye dae?

whit'll—what will   dae—do   dreep—drip   affy—off   dyke—wall
pit—put   oan—on   sterrheid—stairhead   close-wa'—wall of the
entrance-corridor   blooter—smash   chap—knock at   caw—knock
sapsy wean—simpleton child   wulkies—acrobatics   tim—empty
screwtaps—beer-bottles   shauchlin'—shuffling   loaby—lobby
the gemme's a bogey—child's 'game cry', meaning 'The game is forfeit because someone has cheated'.

YOUNG POLITICIAN

What a lovely, lovely moon.
And it's in the constituency too.

THE WORSTEST BEAST

the worstest beast that swims in the sea
is man with his bathing trunks down to his knee

the worstest beast that goes through the air
is man with his comb to tidy his hair

the worstest beast that bores through soil
is man with his uses for metal and oil

the worstest beast that hunts for meat
is man who kills and does not eat

the worstest beast that suckles its young
is man who's scared of nipples and dung

the worstest beast that copulates
is man who's mixed his loves and hates

the worstest beast that has warm skin
is man who stones himself with sin

he's the worstest beast because he's won
it's a master race and it's almost run

PERSON

i have no thumb
i am a little
deformed

i don't wear gloves
but i suffer very much
from the insolence
of those who are thumbed
and find in that
their distinction

JAMES AITCHISON

THE LAST CLEAN BOUGH

Each day that summer he walked the avenue
of elm and hawthorn to the broken orchard.

He put his saw to the dry bough and he thought
of autumns full of fruit, of blossomings.

And he remembered a girl, a night when leaves
moved in the wind and moonlight silvered her.

But that was fifty years ago . . . Now
the house beyond the orchard was a shell.

The orchard wall had fallen stone by stone
and the fruitless trees had fallen: apple, plum,

damson, cherry, pear—the pear tree where
the summer moon had found the silver girl.

The girl beneath the tree beneath the moon
was long since dead. What had they said

that summer night beneath the pear tree where
now he put his saw to the last clean bough?

He shouldered the branch and walked the avenue
of big elms and sparse hawthorn hedge.

In his garden he dropped it on the pile
of timbers stacked against the coming frost.

LANDSCAPE WITH LAPWINGS

It's another April, and a day
with all the seasons in it, with lapwings
falling out of sunlight into rain,
stalling on a squall and then tumbling
over the collapsing wall of air
to float in zones of weightlessness again.

And on a day like this in such a place—
a few square miles of moorland in a round
of rounded hills, rain clouds and scattered trees,
with water flowing clearly over stone—
in such a place I feel the weights slip off
the way a lapwing would if it were me.

The place might form a frame of reference
for calculating weightlessness, and all
the weathers that are in one April day,
for drawing what conclusions can be drawn
from lapwings tumbling in and out of light
with such a total lack of gravity.

CLASSROOM

They feigned maturity, natural defence
against the statelessness of boy-manhood.
And Miss Smith sympathized for she could sense
their insecurity; but each week too she could
see their game become less than pretence,
feel their fear infect her, guess their crude
imaginings. She sweated at the intense
stare that stripped her each week till she stood
naked before them, facing the immense
lust that singed her ageing maidenhood.

222

CHILDREN'S AGES

Aged five, I used to say; aged five, and two.
And then that little stagger of surprise,
like missing the bottom rung of a ladder.
Time passing and time standing still.
Five? And two? How could they have
put on years when I was just the same?

Later I'd sometimes hesitate,
having to think about their ages
and make a quick count of the missing years . . .
Ten and seven, I think. Yes, ten and seven.
Again the little lurch, like falling
through a gap I hadn't known was there.

Now I say eighteen and fifteen, nineteen
and sixteen, twenty and seventeen
without surprise. The years pass faster,
with no missing rungs, no unexpected openings
but like little exercises in perspective
and vanishing point.

THE NEW LIFE

It took him two or three months to work things out—
a smaller flat and car, and the new routes
to work and to the neighbourhood laundrette
and the supermarket with parking space and late
opening, a single bank account
and maintenance for the agreed amount.

Just when he'd got the hang of it and thought
of asking Jane or Emma round for a spot
of supper some night and a drink or two,
a feeling like the aftermath of flu

began to foul things up. Right on the verge
of the new life he found he'd lost the urge.

He had his freedom but he didn't know
what to do with it or where to go.
He scuttered like a drugged rat in a maze
through the twisted orderliness of days
and then went back to sit alone and watch
the television screen grow dim with scotch.

He knew somewhere along the line he'd left
something behind. He tried to think of gifts—
trivial impulsive silly things
they'd given each other in the beginning;
later, they'd handed over gifts that cost
more, to compensate for what they'd lost.

Like flu, this thing would go if he could hold
on for another week or so, he told
himself as he wheeled his trolley up the aisle.
Like flu, he thought. Or love. He stuffed his soiled
shirts in the machine and then sat down
to watch them spinning round and round and round.

IN THE NORTH

Light fades slowly in the long evenings of May and June
here in the north. The eyes adjust
and when I straighten up from a seedbed
I can still make out the darker shapes of the swifts
against an archipelago of clouds
and the outline of a thrush
singing from the top branch of a plum tree.

I feel the stiffness and the aching satisfaction of tasks.
I put the tools away
while I can still see the path to the outhouse.
Indoors, I switch on the light
and begin to wash off the stains of earth and calomel dust.

The thrush calls out and I look from the window
on to an incomprehensible darkness.

I stare until I see the deeper mass
of apple trees and plum trees
and the boundary wall,
black shapes with nothing in between them
except the glint of glass in the greenhouse
and my reflection out there
waiting like another self at ease in the night.

DONALD CAMPBELL

AT A PAIRTY

We observe ane anither cannily owre
the rims o oor respective an separate
distinctions. We keek at
ane anither cautiously atween
the ragged ranges o the thochts
that divide us. For aa that
oor sibnesses are apparent.

Neither o us was invitit here
Baith o us were brocht
Me bi her. You bi him.
We licht oor cigarettes in unison
mind oor drinkan.
We speak when we're spoken tae
an smile when we're tellt.
Neither o us kens the hostess
Neither o us wants tae.

There can be nae touchan o hauns
        nae swappan o smiles.

The distance atween us is great
We try in mony weys tae maister it
Ye throw back yer heid in laughter
an I raise my voice in conversation
—only you dinnae ken my language
        an I dinnae get the joke.

There can be nae touchan o smiles
    nae swappan o hauns.

But aa guid things maun come tae an end
an the knock on the waa maks up its mind
tae thole this nonsense nae further.
Amang the fankle o coats an airms
for ane braithless instant oor shouders
brush, oor smiles touch an oor dreams kiss
in the daurk lobby o oor common want.

GILES GORDON

ELEGY
I. M. Orlando Tobias Gordon
  born Charing Cross Hospital, 5 p.m., 8 August 1967
  died Fulham Hospital, 8 p.m., 8 August 1967

1

For moments she didn't recognize me:
white rubber boots, green coat, mouth and nose pad,
a linen cap. They had me hold her arm,
press a mask to her face to help her breathe.
They strapped her legs up high, covered the limbs
with green leggings, laid green all over her.
She resembled the contours and colours
of distant County Cork, without passion.

The baby when it came was wet and red,
was whisked away from my sight, more so hers,
before colour could be confirmed. (Thank God.)
It lay within its glass case on green cloth,
which also covered its parts. Its colour
was milk chocolate from lack of oxygen.
Green and brown, landscape, equator colours,
surprising pigments for a white baby.

2

Were three hours in this world enough for you?
One hour for each month premature perhaps?
For months you'd swum inside your water sack,
throbbed and banged and made your existence felt.
If you'd stood the pace, waited for three months,
you'd have seen the world. It could wait for you.
There would have been thousands upon thousands
of babies born before you, now to then.
And thousands and thousands of people dead.

Were three hours enough? Is our world so dull
or horrible that you would rather sleep
for all time, having a name and three hours?
Oh how you hurt her, how you have hurt her!
For so long, for such a short time to stay.
I thought you were dead when they drew you out:
you were so silent, no noise, just the mess.
I saw you as you came, your gory head
first, and noticed only baby, not sex
or size. Two hours later I looked again,
having been to Lyons for egg and tea.
You lay in your glass case, breathing wildly
through tubes, and tubes, and tubes; or so it seemed.

And they covered your body and hid you
from me, or what *you* did not wish to see.
Our world is difficult, short of meaning.
If there is a God, then there is a God.
To me you are dead. I am so detached
from you now that I still see you breathing
in your tent, your perfect features so small,
yet a miniature version of a man.
Such perfection could not stand our air long.

3

On the kitchen table, household objects
to do with living: a bread knife and board,
two green saucers, a packet of Corn Flakes,
a saucepan lid; coffee beans, sugar, rice,
lentils and salt in glass jars; cooking oil:
a blue and white striped jug filled with lemon
juice, mixed with water. Half the dead lemon
lies on the table, squeezed, dry and empty.
Also two packets of 'The Iron Tablets',
with instructions: 'Take one tablet with meals,
three times a day throughout your pregnancy:
this is important to ensure that you
do not become anaemic.' And a watch.

On the kitchen table, household objects
to do with dying. The watch has run down.
This still life has been untouched for three days.
There has been no living, only dying
in another place. The Iron Tablets are
an anachronism now, the lemon
and its juice squeezed unnecessarily.
There is no baby. There will not be one.
There was a baby. It breathed for three hours.
All there is to show is her flat stomach,
death and birth certificates, an empty
house. The watch stopped at when the breathing did.
The still life will be still for weeks longer.

DOUGLAS DUNN

LANDSCAPE WITH ONE FIGURE

The shipyard cranes have come down again
To drink at the river, turning their long necks
And saying to their reflections on the Clyde,
'How noble we are.'

The fields are waiting for them to come over.
The trees gesticulate into the rain,
The nerves of grasses quiver at their tips.
Come over and join us in the wet grass!

The wings of gulls in the distance wave
Like handkerchiefs after departing emigrants.
A tug sniffs up the river, looking like itself.
Waves fall from their small heights on river mud.

If I could sleep standing, I would wait here
Forever, become a landmark, something fixed
For tug crews or seabound passengers to point at,
An example of being a part of a place.

SHIPS

When a ship passes at night on the Clyde,
The swans in the reeds picking the oil from their feathers
Look up at the lights, the noise of new waves,
Against hill-climbing houses, malefic cranes.

A fine rain attaches itself to the ship like skin.
The lascars play poker, the Scottish mate looks
At the last lights, that one is Ayrshire,
Others on lonely rocks, or clubfooted peninsulas.

They leave restless boys without work in the river towns.
In their houses are fading pictures of fathers ringed
Among ships' complements in wartime, model destroyers,
Souvenirs from uncles deep in distant engine rooms.

Then the boys go out, down streets that look on water.
They say, 'I could have gone with them,'
A thousand times to themselves in the glass cafés,
Over their American soft drinks, into their empty hands.

THE LOVE DAY

April, and young women glorify their flesh.
Their blushes warm their lovers' eyes.

The frisky toughs discard their heavy jackets,
Put on dark, sparse muscle-shirts.

Youth walks in couples nervous to cool bedrooms.
Some learn that love is not bad or permanent.

The ruffians are soft with their girlfriends.
They smile, keep their voices down, park their motorbikes.

Spring, the fugitives come to a stop here,
The thrush muffles its voice under the blossom,

Young husbands notice the flower shops,
The old men kiss their wives and long for their children.

It only lasts a day. After it, the insects come out.
Tender hands and mouths go back to eating.

THE NEW GIRLS

The dancing and drinking go on into the night
In the rooms of Edwardian houses,
In flats that cads and fashionable young couples rent,
Where the parties of Saturday happen
After the pub everyone goes to has closed.

There are always the girls there no one's seen before,
Who soon become known and their first names
    remembered.
Replacing the girls who 'simply just vanished'
To new jobs in London or husbands who've quietened
    down.

The new girls leave with the men who brought them
To rooms nearby in the same district, or one just like it.
At dawn, three streets from their homes,
The girls leave cars with doors that slam,
Engines that sound like men's contemptuous laughter,
As they disappear at fifty down an empty street.

Then they reach the door, and turn the key, and know
They have been listening to their own footsteps
In the silence of Sunday before the milkmen,
When the cats are coming home to eat, and water dripping
From the bridge is heard a hundred yards away.

THE HARP OF RENFREWSHIRE
Contemplating a map

Annals of the trilled R, gently stroked L,
Lamenting O of local literature,
Open, on this, their one-page book, a still
Land-language chattered in a river's burr.

Small-talk of herdsmen, rural argument—
These soft disputes drift over river-meadows,
A darg of conversations, a verbal scent—
Tut-tutted discourse, time of day, word-brose.

Named places have been dictionaried in
Ground's secret lexicon, its racial moan
Of etymology and cries of pain
That slit a summer wind and then were gone.

A mother calls her daughter from her door.
Her house, my stone illusion, hugs its hill.
From Eaglesham west to the rocky shore
Her cry is stretched across bog-asphodel.

The patronymic miles of grass and weddings,
Their festivals of gender, covenants,
Poor pre-industrially scattered steadings,
Ploughed-up davochs—old names, inhabitants.

And on my map is neither wall or fence,
But men and women and their revenue,
As, watching them, I utter into silence
A granary of whispers rinsed in dew.

WAR BLINDED

For more than sixty years he has been blind
Behind that wall, these trees, with terrible
Longevity wheeled in the sun and wind
On pathways of the soldiers' hospital.

For half that time his story's troubled me—
That showroom by the ferry, where I saw
His basketwork, a touch-turned filigree
His fingers coaxed from charitable straw;

Or how he felt when young, enlisting at
Recruiting tables on the football pitch,
To end up slumped across a parapet,
His eye-blood running in a molten ditch;

Or how the light looked when I saw two men,
One blind, one in a wheelchair, in that park,
Their dignity, which I have not forgotten,
Which helps me struggle with this lesser dark.

That war's too old for me to understand
How he might think, nursed now in wards of want,
Remembering that day when his right hand
Gripped on the shoulder of the man in front.

ALAN BOLD

THE REALM OF TOUCHING

Between my lips the taste of night-time blends
And then dissolves. It is blank as my eyelids close.
For a flickering of time I concentrate on how time ends.

It should be present, the scent of the rose
We bought, though one petal has begun to fall.
Somehow that simplifies the girl I chose.

Night music must be the sweetest sound of all.
It is made to overwhelm with virtuosity.
But every night it is the same pounding on the same wall.

Nocturnal images are said to be the ones that stay
Longest, with exploitation of the dark half-tone.
This I disregard and watch for the day.

A touch in the realm of touching alone
Adds presence to the absence of light.
A clasp of hands, then bodies, my own
And hers is when I welcome the blindness of night.

SHORE

Sheets of water are washed out on the shore as
The sea bubbles, seems to boil then sends
Gouts of spray steaming in towards the land.
End-on the waves brighten to reveal
Fantastic swaying columns of suspended seaweed
Whose loose luxuriant curls of brown and red
Are smashed against a tepid sandstone bed.
There is a ferocious crash, and then a pause
Before the sea provides its own applause.

DEATH'S-HEAD MOTH

I saw it settle like a stain
On the dusk, each tired wing
Spread flat upon the window pane

Yet the angles were less than bad,
The design of its parts persuasive,
So I picked up a sketching pad,

Traced out the furtive symmetry,
Coaxed light round furred edges,
And wondered why it disgusted me,

It lacked the frenetic sly
Grace and rainbow hues
Of the madcap buttefly.

THE OLD BING

A century ago deep dripping galleries were gutted
To build this monument above the wooded carse;
Now the bing is overwhelmed by dog-rose and bramble,
Veins of wild strawberry throb under bracken.

In winter keen hill winds and valley rains
Strip it bare revealing a gaunt memorial;
Stark in its grandeur the bing rears from the carse
Like the tumulus of a long-dead jarl or thane.

At its base a slow river ambles reflecting tall
Hills and still herons heraldic in twilight;
Not even the sighs of evening winds can recall
The anguished grunts of those nameless toilers

Who hacked a sparse living from grudging seams,

Cursed at roof-falls, mourned lost comrades,
Indifferent as moles to the cenotaph above them
Each day darkly rising, shouldering the sun.

TOM LEONARD

STORM DAMAGE

There is a stain on the ceiling above the bed.
Rainwater. A relic of last year's storm.
It is roughly circular. Darkest at the centre.
The perimeter is not clearly defined.

Eclipse. Your body moves on mine.
Your face looks down on me.
The lips are smiling. The stain
Becomes a halo round your head.

My mind goes back twelve years.
I am a child again, lying in the grass,
Staring into the sky. Eclipse.

You ask me what I'm thinking.

FEED MA LAMZ

Doon nyir hungkirz. Wheesht.

    nay fornirz ur communists
    nay langwij
    nay lip
    nay laffn ina sunday
    nay g.b.h. (septina wawr)
    nay nooky huntn
    nay tea-leaven
    nay chanty rasslin
    nay nooky huntn nix doar
    nur kuvitn thir ox

Oaky doaky. Stick way it
—rahl burn thi lohta yiz.

Authentic? Joyce *authentic?* I'll tell you.
I mind well when I was about twelve, we went
to a mission. The school that is. Our Lady of
Lourdes, Cardonald. Anyway. There was this *atmosphere*
you could have cut it with a knife. It was like the
way you felt turning up when you hadn't done your
homework, only this was a *crowd* feeling. Guilt
and terror. Awful. And this missionary was going
on about how he was fed up with boys coming to
confess about their turty habits and turty chokes.
Big pause. KATLIX ME OI! Thump. KATLIX ME OI!
                                                    Well,
anyway, I mind when I went home, my father was sitting
on the left of the fireplace, my mother on the right.
We went to the mission today, and got a sermon, I said.
What was the sermon about, said my mother. It was about
a new sin called impurity, I said. Oh, said my mother,
looking past my shoulder, it's not new . . .

THE VOYEUR

what's your favourite word dearie
is it wee
I hope it's wee
wee's such a nice wee word
like a wee hairy dog
with two wee eyes
such a nice wee word to play with dearie
you can say it quickly
with a wee smile
and a wee glance to the side
or you can say it slowly dearie
with your mouth a wee bit open
and a wee sigh dearie

236

a wee sigh
put your wee head on my shoulder dearie
oh my
a great wee word
and Scottish
it makes you proud

CHRISTOPHER RUSH

SEABIRDS

The brash gull scrawls its signature
across the screeching slate of the bay,
and has much to say
(or so it seems)
to the brute rocks.

The poised gannet's gormandizing plume
makes a much more efficient mark,
plummeting through the dark
waters, after contracts
from illiterate fish.

Even the deep heron's studious stance
appears a strange understanding
after all, on only one foot standing,
as if showing off
to the dumb sand.

But the still cormorant's humble sign of the cross,
as in unwritten places it stretches gospel-wings,
to the changing sea-pages brings
a wise detachment:
devouring time.

237

HER PLACE

My rival's house
is peopled with many surfaces.
Ormolu and gilt, slipper satin,
lush velvet couches,
cushions so stiff you can't sink in,
tables polished clear enough to see distortions in.

We take our shoes off at her door,
shuffle on stocking feet, softshoe, tiptoe—the parquet
    floor
is beautiful and its surface must
be protected. Dust-
cover, drawn shade
won't let the surface colours fade.

Silver sugar tongs and silver salver,
my rival serves us tea.
She glosses over him and me.
I'm all edges, all surface, a shell
and yet my rival thinks she means me well.
Oh what swims beneath her surface I can tell.
Soon, my rival—
capped tooth, varnished nail—
will fight foul for her survival.
Daughterly, deferential I sip
and thank her nicely for each bitter cup.

And I have much to thank her for.
The son she bore
(first blood to her)
never never never will escape scot free
from the sour pot luck of family.
And oh how close
the family that furnishes my rival's house.
Great succubus.
Queen bee.

She is far more unconscious,
far more dangerous than me.
Listen, I was always my own worst enemy.
She has taken even this from me.

She dishes up her dreams at breakfast.
Dinner and her salt tears pepper our soup.
She won't give up.

POEM FOR MY SISTER

My little sister likes to try my shoes,
to strut in them,
admire her spindle-thin twelve-year-old legs
in this season's styles.
She says they fit her perfectly,
but wobbles
on their high heels, they're
hard to balance.

I like to watch my little sister
playing hopscotch,
admire the neat hops-and-skips of her,
their quick peck,
never-missing their mark, not
over-stepping the line.
She is competent at peever.

I try to warn my little sister
about unsuitable shoes,
point out my own distorted feet, the callouses,
odd patches of hard skin.
I should not like to see her
in *my* shoes.
I wish she could stay
sure footed,
                    sensibly shod.

NOISES IN THE DARK *(Anatolia, April 1974)*

The four a.m. call to the faithful wakes us,
its three-times off-key harmony of drones and wails.
Above our head I snap the lightcord but the power fails
as usual, leaving us in the dark. Tomorrow takes us
who knows where. What ruins? What towns? What smells?
Nothing shakes us.
We touch and today's too painful sunburn sticks and sears
apart again. Faithful to something three long years
no fear, no final foreign dark quite breaks us.

Hotel habitués,
the ritually faithful wash their feet. Old plumbing
    grumbles.
The tap-leak in our rust-ringed basin tickles
irritant, incessant, an inch out of the dark. Whitewash
    crumbles
from the wall where the brittle cockroach trickles.
Fretful, faithful, wide to the dark, can we ever forget
this shabby town hotel, the shadow of the minaret?
Human or bird or animal? What was it cried?
The dark smear across our wall still unidentified.

TAM LIN'S LADY

'O I forbid you maidens a'
who wear gowd in your hair—
to come or go to Carterhaugh
for young Tam Lin is there.'

So you met him in a magic place?
O.K.
But that's a bit airy fairy for me.
I go for the specific—you could, for instance,
say that when he took you for a coffee
before he stuck you on the last bus
there was one of those horrible congealed-on
plastic tomatoes on the table . . . oh don't

240

ask me
I don't know why everything has to be so sordid these
      days . . .
I can take *some* sentiment
tell me how charmed you were
when he wrote both your names and a heart in spilt
      coffee—
anything except that he carved them on the eldern tree.
But have it your own way.
Picking apart your personal
dream landscape of court and castle and greenwood
isn't really up to me.
So call it magical. A fair country.
Anyway you were warned.

And if, as the story goes
nine times out of ten—
he took you by the milkwhite hand & by the grassgreen
      sleeve
& laid you on the bonnie bank & asked of you no leave,
well, so what?
You're not the first to fall for it,
good green girdle and all—
with your schooltie rolled up in your pocket
trying to look eighteen. I know.
All perfectly forgiveable.
Relax.

What I do think was a little dumb
if only you'd trust him just this once
was to swallow that old one about you being
the only one who could save him.

Oh I see—there was this lady
he couldn't get free of.
Seven years and more he said he'd sacrificed himself
and if you didn't help him he'd end up
a fairy for ever! Enslaved.

Or worse still in hell without you.
Well, well.
So he stopped you from wandering in the forest
and picking pennyroyal and foxgloves
and making appointments and borrowing money for the
    abortion.
He said all would be well
if only you'd trust him just this once
and go through
what he was honest enough to admit in advance
would be hell and highwater for you.
So he told you which relatives to pander to
and which to ignore.
How to snatch him from the Old One
and hold on through thick and thin
through every change that happened.
Oh but it was terrible!
It seemed earlier, you see,
he'd been talking in symbols (like
adder-snake, wild savage bear
brand of bright iron red-hot from the fire)
and as usual the plain unmythical truth was worse.
At any rate you were good and brave, you did
hang on, hang on tight.
And in the end of course
everything turned out conventionally right
with the old witch banished to her corner lamenting,
cursing his soft heart and the fact she couldn't keep him,
and everyone sending out for booze for the wedding.

So we're all supposed to be happy?
But how about you, my fallen fair maiden
now the drama's over, tell me
how goes the glamourie?
After the twelve casks of good claret wine
and the twelve and twelve of muskadine,
tell me
what about you?
How do you think Tam Lin will take
all the changes you go through?

SEA PIECE

The night pries at a window.
It fingers the wooden frames
till rotten splinters drop away.

Go back, there is no-one here,
no girl newly risen from the wave,
her skin painted like a sea-plane.

She is out on the barren shore.
She questions the north,
asking, who ploughed it with salt?

It's not just in history, the fields
spoiled by brine, this same hour
a lover goes to bed with his wife.

WE MEET AGAIN

For the first time in seven years
we meet.
Your son says to my daughter
'I hate girls: go away.'
She smiles her formidable smile.
Fates get their yarn in a twist.

They'll wait.
While he swings on his tarzan rope
or casts a new lure in the sea,
she'll hang back from her brothers
till she can make this fellow
look for the land he first came from.

Who will remember today
when they discover
their own surprising Eden?
As, in the pretty far back,
once it was you and me.

243

DEERHOUNDS

Admit the lives more valuable
than our life, than the bodies we bear
more beautiful: tall grey dogs,

what huntsman, what dogboy loosed you
on our slow hearts
and let you slaughter them?

Long dogs, you move with air
belling the vault of your ribcage.
You subdue the miles below your hocks.

Levelled out in speed across wayless country,
over the open grassmoor that is paradise,
the onset of your going undulates the ground.

The bracken hurdles below your height,
the rushes make way for you;
your hard eyes hold in sight the rapid hills.

Brace of deerhounds, a matched two!
Intent, all flame, is what quickens
those long throats thonged with leather.

INFERTILITY PATIENT

'I could never have enough children.' Katherine Mansfield

To lift another woman's child
is like carrying a bundle of barbed wire.
And one who will let himself be held
stirs every bereaved desire.

Between collarbone and breast
his hard head makes an impression:
a dent in a white quilt
someone's secretly been sleeping on.

244

My hands fall empty in my lap
when she lifts him away.
I can share, as I give him up,
only his backwards look with no wave.

She's the fertile one while I am not.
Inject a dye and see my tubes are drawn
blocked and scarred, death's first print I've got
in me: you month, rat's jaw, I see you yawn.

AT THE FALLS OF CLYDE

The dipper bird
the freshwater-wet bird
swims
with stubby wings.

The waterfall drops
in a slender stream
falls
a curtain of water.

Whitethroat like foam
on fastflowing stream
the dipper flies
directly into the waterfall.

Watching for the way
he walks along the bottom
your eyes ache
all stream-slippery.

THE OLD WOMAN'S REEL

She is at the small deep window
looking through and out;

245

the Aran islands, rock and seawater,
lie all about.
A face strong in poverty's hauteur
is hers, then and now.

Being a young woman in Flaherty's film
'Man of Aran',
she nearly drowned in the undertow
by the boat where she ran.
He kept on filming even though
he thought her dead on the rockrim.

A body plaited by water twine
they carried ashore:
partnered in the ocean's set dance
by two men or more.
The sea had had its chance
to peel her off by the shoreline.

Now in her great old age
toothless and tough,
the island music still delights her:
one dance is not enough.
The tunes of a people poor and cut off there
have a special power to engage.

Drawn upright, her stiff bones
already dancing,
she spins, not on one foot
but on her stick, tap-balancing.
While to one side like a pliant offshoot
a little girl mimics her, unbeknown.

ANDREW GREIG

SAPPER

Yard by yard I let you
sap my resistance
and undermine
my easy independence.

Your smiles and warm ways
burrowed burning
into my cool brain; your firmness
honeycombed my heart.

Then you laid in
barrel-loads of love
and laid a powder trail
to the ammunition dump

of my desire. And now
I've caught you, hand
on my fuse. And I say
'Yes, love'.

THE GLOVE

This room need not speak of her.
It is enough
the air is hard to breathe.

On the table, a flattened glove.
Nothing has moved
since she slipped out.

There is no calling from kitchen or shore.

For a ghost as subtle as a lack
there are rituals of banishment
in time:

vacuums are filled, rooms aired,
furniture shifted, walls painted,
a new lodger—

and one day the glove is gone
edged out of this world
as things are when we have no room

even for their absence.

IN GALLOWAY

In Galloway the drystane dykes that curl
like smoke over the shoulder of the hill
are built with holes
through which sky shows and spindrift birds,
so the wind is baffled but not barred
lest drifting snow smoors a sheltering herd.

There is an art in framing holes
and in the space between the stones.
Structures pared to the bone—
the line that pleases by what's not there
or drydykes laced across the whirling air.

ROBERT CRAWFORD

COLL
for V.T.H.H.

Imagine an asylum for anemometers,
A discotheque of water.

Horizontal sleet on the west of Coll
Scours the headlands. Tattered crofts
Lie like stone litter that will not rot

On voes and machair. Trespassing through
A frameless window with the wind's white grit
Against me like shot of God's anger

I photograph what I wish to show you
Purged of that air. The lens is rainlogged.
My hand is cold to the bone,

But this matters because it sets the limits
All understand. One small lit square,
Chaos made dumb by a window.

FOUND POEM

I found a cassette unwound in a hedge,
The casing smashed, only the tape was left,
And I followed it with my fingers,
A smooth kind of talking grass.

You could not play it, except as a game
Of hide and seek. Rewind, fast forward, record
Had no meaning now, Beethoven stuck
In privet, Pink Floyd caught live

In hawthorn blossom. Even if I wound it
All around my fingers, bound in sound,
There's no machine would take it.
Had someone so hated the SNO

That he'd flung them out of a moving car?
Or maybe a child had tried to find
Whether *La Mer* was as long as Brownside Road.
I thought of ragged parsons finding

Sermons in stones, of overgrown words
In country churchyards, the vox pop sound of silence.
The whole thing might have been packed with poems.
Anyhow, I only found this one.

DUNOON

Mist becomes polythene we burst with our fingers.
Along the coastline hills are wrapped up.
Tomatoes, leeks. The country is on a level
With these things. Tugging our cold thumbs,

Petulantly pleading, love
Cannot replace shopping or the mending of telephones.
Accelerating away behind tinted windows,
The chairman drafts a long letter.

THE SCOTTISH NATIONAL CUSHION SURVEY

Our heritage of Scottish cushions is dying.
Teams of careful young people on training schemes
Arrived through a government incentive, counting
Every cushion. In Saltcoats, through frosty Lanark.
They even searched round Callanish
For any they'd missed. There are no more Scottish cushions
Lamented the papers. Photographs appeared
Of the last cushion found in Gaeldom.
Silk cushions, pin cushions, pulpit cushions.
We must preserve our inheritance.
So the museums were built: The Palace of Cushions, the
    National
Museum of Soft Seating, and life went on elsewhere
Outside Scotland. The final Addendum was published
Of *Omnes Pulvini Caledonii.*
Drama documentaries. A chapter closed.
And silently in Glasgow quick hands began
Angrily making cushions.